Unveiling the Mystery of
Life and Death

Unveiling the Mystery of
Life and Death

DR. SYLVIE DANIEL BIDOT

COVER PHOTO PORTRAIT AND PHOTOS " ONLY YOU " ON PAGE #5 AND " LIFE IS A RAINBOW OF EXPERIENCES" PAGE # 157 WERE TAKEN BY THE AWARD WINNING PHOTOGRAPHER ALLEN PATROU OF PHOENIX ARIZONA.

www.apatrouphotography.com
email: info@apatrouphotography.com

Back cover picture taken in the Dominican Republic by Valentina Bidot

Library of Congress Control Number: 2007905517
ISBN: Hardcover   978-1-4257-6821-8
                      Softcover   978-1-4257-6810-2

This book was printed in the United States of America.

To order additional copies of this book, contact:
Xlibris Corporation
1-888-795-4274
www.Xlibris.com
Orders@Xlibris.com

37187

"Only You"

The Sounds of Flying Dreams

To the memory of my parents,
Louis and Luigina Daniel.

To my first teachers, who provided me with
a wonderful and superb life from the very
beginning. I thank you for giving me the spring
of love and guidance, shaping me into the person
that I am today. Mom, you have taught me how
to be a compassionate mother, and devoted
wife. Father, you have taught me that life has
no boundaries and the sky is limitless.

My thanks go to all children of the universe. Their unconditional love brings light to the negated and dark world and leads to God's kingdom.

FOREWORD

In life's episodes, we come to know how rich its experiences are, drawing from our intimate human relations, seeking to know all about our triumphs and defeats.

Nestled in the confines of our experiences, we are prompted to display the height of our accomplishments and victories and explore the depths of our disappointments and retreats.

Ridden by a misfortune, one has no alternative but to follow its course and track its deep roots, enabling one to discover the linchpin of truth that overrides and underscores the whole of existence.

In her triumphant journey, Dr. Sylvie Bidot depicts in her book the story of her life. She concludes that God is man's polestar. It is He who guides His children to the path of inner illumination, lifts them up when they stumble, and takes them out of the net they have been trapped, into the lofty realms of spiritual fulfillment.

Despite the set of difficult times and hardships that Sylvie experienced and \despite the harsh vicissitudes she faced, she was able to endure all grief and sorrowful events.

Armed with a strong will, she decided to overcome the tragic event that befell her, inspired by the illumined truth, a truth affirming God's presence in us, who favors us with His numerous graces and unconditional love.

In a very moving step, Sylvie shows the way out of the depths of her despair and deep sorrow and pain resulting from the loss of two of her dearly beloved ones.

Sylvie's journey is our journey too, a journey crowned by the teachings of illumined minds and inspired by the spiritual teachings of the souls who preceded us. It is a journey that makes our burden lighter and alleviates the lesser cross that is destined for us all, to carry it willingly and courageously.

Sylvie's journey is an ideal lesson for many of us who are doomed to live as she did and experience the tragic event in which she was able, finally, to overcome and rise up from the ashes like the legendary phoenix.

Sylvie's journey is the revelation of God's image in us all, who, through our illumined faith, liberates us from life's illusions and tragedies—including death, the mother of all tragedies.

Dr. Paul B. Mohr Jr.

PREFACE

This book is a product of much work and research related to life and death. It is my wish to make a worthwhile addition to what has been written by others in this field. The subject of life and death causes mankind to reflect on unanswered questions, such as Why did this happen? What is the purpose of one's life on this earth? What is the purpose of death? etc. Through the death and loss of my mother and son twenty years ago, I have found the answers to many such questions. In order to do this, I had to connect with my Creator through deep meditation. Thru my higher consciousness, I was able to talk to God and discover the reasons for this tragedy and what my purpose in this life is. The average human being cannot help a person or ease his or her pain when losing a child. Losing a child is like losing a part of oneself. Only by connecting with my higher consciousness and talking to my Creator was I able to discover that there is no separation between us and our departed loved ones. We are all one. And because of my discovery, I feel I can help others going through grief and loss.

Acknowledgment

My gratitude, appreciation, and devotion is dedicated to the Omnipresent, who guided me with illumined grace and bestowed on me the strength to stand life's hardships and difficulties. His eternal love guided me to the path of my beloved guru, Paramahansa Yogananda. His teachings awakened my soul and dispelled my doubts and false ideas.

My greatest appreciation and love goes to my mother and father for providing me with a great beginning in the first chapter of my life and for giving me a wonderful sister and two brothers. All of them encouraged me with lots of support and love. I would also like to give my heartfelt thanks to my friend and life partner in all walks of life, my other half and only sweetheart, my husband Robert. He has always been the solid rock in times of hardship. The road of life is long and hard, but together, with God's will, all will be well. The Omnipotent will be watching over us.

I am also indebted to my two angels, my wonderful children Richard and Valentina. To Ricky goes all my motherly love, for he is my teacher and my guardian angel whose soul ever looks after me. I miss you, dear Ricky, but I know well that you did see to it that I looked for truth and the light, the keys that link us with the cosmic power. It was you who led my faltering steps and taught me how to live in the light. You helped me realize that there is no separation. We have always been together and shall always be. Your physical body is gone, but our love unites us with the eternal. "I love you and you shall ever live in my mind."

I am indebted to my sweet angel Valentina. You are the sun that ever shines on every moment of my life. You are the wondrous example of true love. Your gleaming smile tells how beautiful God is. You are my earthly life, my dream of tomorrow, and my eternal life.

Your soul is so joyous due to your utter belief that the Omnipresent is in you. You, therefore, give love and life force to whomever you touch. You showered me with torrential flow of love after Ricky passed away. It was you who made me certain of the light that I have found. Thank you, my angel. May the Omniscient always bless you and ever keep your path lit.

My deepest gratitude to my beloved daughter, Valentina. For your hard work, creativity, encouragement, support, and for the many hours spent editing and organizing the manuscript.

Special thanks to my exceptional friend Noel Abdulahad for your endless encouragement and assistance in organizing, and editing the original manuscript.

Many thanks to my darling and wonderful niece Venus Sahwany. Your editorial suggestions were most valuable.

My thanks and gratitude go to my dearest friend Mr. Allen Patrou the award winning photographer, who captured thru his artistic eye, the essence of my true feelings.

I

On a beautiful summer evening, I was outside in the garden. The only sound I heard was the falling water from the fountain and the chirping of the crickets. The only thing that emanated light was the smiling face of the moon and a blanket of twinkling diamonds. The flapping wings of an angel created a light breeze that caressed my face and played with my long hair. The roses of the garden were moving. A sweet, intoxicating smell suffused the air, and I realized then that the angel had delicately touched the roses. They were sharing God's beautiful creation with me. Suddenly, a wave of powerful energy swept me off my feet, transposed me to a place beyond this world, where I saw everything in a clear vision. I understood what true love is.

From these heights, I saw the world's highest mountains covered with snow. They looked happy, radiant, and pure like brides on their wedding day. They wore long white gowns and long veils, waiting for their grooms to unveil them and give them the first kiss after exchanging their vows. The mountains waited for the sun to shine to melt the snow and reveal the long overdue green grass. I gazed at the earth with a deeper look. I saw a great sea of gold swinging like a dancer from one side to another. Clad with a long flared golden dress, it danced to the melody of the *Blue Danube* (by Strauss). Suddenly, I realized that the sea of gold was the field of wheat moving with the rhythm of the angels whispering, "God is great."

I looked behind me, and I saw the majestic ocean; and on its shore, I caught sight of a tall, strong-built young man.

"Oh my god, is that you, Richard? I have not seen you in ten years."

Suddenly, I found myself going back in time to March of 1972. It was the day my son was born. Birth is the miracle of life. All night, I had been in labor. I counted the seconds. It was my first child, and my first experience going into labor and feeling the ever-present lingering pain all over my body. I did not know what to do or how to get rid of the pain. The minutes became hours; the hours were like days and the night seemed eternal. I thought, *Dear God, give me strength to endure this pain.*

I started talking to my baby. Maybe he would soothe my pain. What did I know about childbirth? I had no clue of what to expect. I was nineteen years old. One thing I knew was that soon I would have a beautiful son, and at that moment, I went into a trance. I saw myself sitting in a garden fledged with greenery, a rainbow of colored roses, and canopylike trees. I felt as though God was embracing me. At a distance, I saw the majestic mountains touching heaven and a powerful, intense waterfall pouring down millions of thin silver and gold ribbons. The earth and heavens merged into one unit to form this garden of Eden. There was no separation; all is one and one is all (God). In the stillness of my mind, I was looking at the beauty surrounding me. I perceived a silhouette of an angel emerging from the waterfall and approaching me. Enormous light gushed forth from the angel's outstretched arms.

The nearer the angel came, the more peaceful and joyful I felt. Sweet fragrance filled the atmosphere. A bright light embraced me, and the angel spoke to me, "With God's love and light, I hand you your son Richard. He will bring you great joy, peace, and harmony; and above all, he will open the door for you to know that there is no separation. We are all part of the whole, and we all come from the light. Richard will be the one to give you this experience. Love him, for *he* is your teacher in this lifetime." I looked at the baby and held him in my arms. It was like holding the universe. I forgot the pain, the stress, the confusion. It seemed as though he was the perfect cure for all the discomfort I went through. The chill in my body was replaced by the warmth of my baby's body.

The tears in my eyes turned into tears of joy. Taking a long look at his eyes, I felt my life was transformed. A tremendous wave of love and compassion consigned me to a world filled with harmony and light. This beautiful soul touched me like I had never been touched before.

I couldn't believe it; what a wonderful experience it was—birth and life. I thought, *Dear God, I am so fortunate—a little child in my arms. He was me, not just a part of me.* I glanced at his little glowing face emanating with so much love. I touched his head, thinking of his brain, a brain of a genius; his mind and heart, a mind of a peacemaker and the heart of a lion who fears nothing and no one but God. I looked into his eyes, the eyes that can only see the light. I looked at his delicate ears, the ears that would always listen to nature and life's symphonies. I glanced at his perfect mouth, and I knew he would always spell out nothing but words of wisdom. I looked at his arms and hands and saw in them the arms and hands of a life builder. I touched his fingers; these perfect tender fingers would always point to God's perfect creation. I checked his legs and lenient feet, and I knew that these legs would always walk the extra mile to help others and spread love amongst all people and share God's teachings with mankind. Then I came to realize that he was not only my son, but my guardian angel. "Oh, dear God, what have I done to deserve this perfect and precious gift from you? What a miracle! I promise to take good care of this treasure."

My mother's angelic voice, asking me how I was feeling, brought me back to the physical plane. The nurse was standing, watching the monitor to see if I was getting closer to delivering my baby. At the same time, my mother was trying to distract me from the pain by talking to me and telling me to breathe the proper way. She was holding my hand and launching forth all the love a human can give.

I realized how important mothers are in a child's life. My mother taught me everything I know in this life. She was the foundation of my human experience. She had been the most important person in my life I could ever remember. Her love to all of us was boundless, unconditional, and undivided. She was an example of patience, harmony, understanding, compassion, and forgiveness. She was our lifeline. She had always been my best friend. During all my difficulties, she helped me immensely to be wise and strong. She made me realize where to lead my steps forth. Some experiences imposed on me much pain and disappointment. Some others brought me happiness and joy.

She always advised me in her kind way to be an expert player in life's game. Mistakes happen, and I have to accept and learn from them. We are here to learn. None of us is perfect. In achieving perfection, one needs to experience difficulties. That is how we test our ability to learn and overcome our imperfections. The only way to make us conscious beings is by using the free gifts that God gave us, his wisdom and his intelligence. I am so grateful to God that I had a mother full of love and compassion.

My mother and father have been a great example for us on how to live our lives, now and tomorrow. My mother showed her love in everything she did—helping my father, hand in hand, to raise us, keeping the house clean and shapely, cooking delectable meals, helping us understand our homework, and surprising us on our birthdays. She was an excellent person with a beautiful soul. My mind floods with lots of wonderful memories of our life together, a life full of love, understanding, and respect. I learned to be grateful for everything and everybody—most of all, to God who gave us the opportunity to experience ourselves in the physical plane.

Again, her angelic voice and her tender touch caressed my face. She looked passionately into my eyes and said that my husband had just called and that he would be flying in on standby from his business trip. I replied, "That's great! I wish him to be here when the baby is born." She said, "By the will of God." Suddenly, I felt cold and exhausted. I told my mother that I would like to take some time to rest. She replied, "Sleep with angels. Sleep, sweet soul."

I drifted away to another world to find my mother and my son holding in their hands the book of *The Prophet* by Kahlil Gibran. Together, they read to me:

> You have sung to me in my aloneness, and I of your longings have built a tower in the sky.

> But now our sleep has fled and our dream is over, and it is no longer dawn.

> The noontide is upon us and our half walking has turned to fuller day, and we must part.

> If in the twilight of memory we should meet once more, we shall speak again together and you shall sing to me a deeper song.

> And if our hands should meet in another dream, we shall build another tower in the sky.

Then I saw myself reading back to them from the same book:

And she hailed him, saying:

Prophet of God, in quest of the uttermost, long have
you searched the distances for your ship.

And now your ship has come, and you must needs go.

Deep is your longing for the land of your memories and
the dwelling place of your greater desires; and our
love would not bind you nor our needs hold you.

Yet this we ask ere you leave us, that you speak to
us and give us of your truth.

And we will give it unto our children, and they unto
their children, and it shall not perish.

In your aloneness you have watched with our days,
and in your wakefulness, you have listened to the
weeping and the laughter of our sleep.

Now therefore disclose us to ourselves, and tell us all
that has been shown you of that which is between
birth and death.

Both replied, reading from *The Prophet*:

> You would know the secret of death.
>
> But how shall you find it unless you seek it in the heart of life?
>
> The owl whose night-bound eyes are blind unto the day cannot unveil the mystery of light.
>
> If you would indeed behold the spirit of death, open your heart wide unto the body of life.
>
> For life and death are one, even as the river and the sea are one.

A moment of silence broke out, and then both of them looked straight into my eyes and said to me, "Out of your experience, go on and help others. Teach them the truth about life and death."

The voice of my husband saying, "Honey, I am home," delivered me from my trance.

I was born in Haifa to a father and a mother from different backgrounds, a Lebanese father and an Italian mother.

The foundation of this family was based on love, compassion, understanding, and respect. These qualities have been planted in us since birth. It was a way of life for us. I was the oldest. My sister is younger than me, and my two brothers are younger than my sister.

Our family did everything together. We went together to church on Sundays, traveled together, went on picnics together, did projects together, and always ate together. We were a very close-knit family. My father was a well-known and respected architect. We, his children, became used to the attention and recognition by others. We felt secure and confident because of what my mom and dad procured for us in terms of comfort and security while we were growing up. I loved our life as a family so much that I could not wait to graduate from high school and meet some nice man and get married. I wanted a higher education. I wanted to be as important and famous as my father, but the idea of being married and having children, living in a happy home and a warm environment, was the strong desire that was impressed on my subconscious. I wanted a family just like my parents had. Perhaps this was because I was the oldest or because I grew up in a happy home. Nevertheless, I wanted the same for myself.

When I was in my eleventh grade, I met a nice gentleman. He played in the band at my uncle's wedding reception. He seemed to be very respectful and discrete in letting me know that I was his bride-to-be. He introduced me to the members of his family who were also at the wedding: "Ms. Sylvie Daniel, the daughter of the famous architect Mr. Louis Daniel." His family appeared to be very loving and caring.

Later I found out they were a very well-known family in town too. My feelings at that moment were feelings of joy and satisfaction. Deep in my heart, I felt they were a very nice family. They cared about one another, and that was important to me. However, I had some concerns about my feelings, but I overlooked them. The more I got to know him, the more I saw he was a loving and generous person, and I got along very well with his family. I continued my education, and we got married after I graduated from high school. I was no longer a miss, but Mrs. I had a home and a husband. Soon my guardian angel, my son Ricky, arrived. I now had everything. My life was full and complete. I had the family life I wanted, but it didn't last.

Nine months after Ricky's birth, the concerns I had resurfaced. My husband was not the gentleman I thought he was. We were too young. The relationship died. In the beginning, it was the birth of the relationship; and a few months later, that relationship came to an end. It was both our faults. The first challenge I faced was being a single parent. What had been once "the past" is now over. I had to go on and face the first challenge of my adulthood. The relationship was dead. I had a baby beside myself. I could be strong. I was in the here and now, and I had to continue my journey. I must learn how to face failure, disappointment, rejection, and the feeling of being lonely. I was used to living with compassion, understanding, and respect. All of these moral traits went out the window in my relationship. I had to face the people, the culture that I came from, the background, the mentality, the judgment.

I had to face my parents, remembering their advice for me to get a higher education and forget about marriage at such a young age. Even though I was reluctant to get married, I took that path. My parents loved me enough to give me a choice. When I went home and told my mom and dad about the situation, I perceived the deep pain in their eyes because from the beginning, they wanted to spare me all frustration and blighted hopes.

Sometimes in life, we have to learn the hard way. I realized my responsibility toward my child and toward myself. So I started one day at a time to organize my thoughts and deal with the unbelievable rejection and the loss. It would not be easy to find my place in a judgmental society. I knew that I chose this path, and now I had to find a new path that would fit me for the rest of my life. My first marriage was a big challenge for me. I now needed something positive to take place in my life. My self-esteem and self-worth had suffered a tremendous shock. I decided to do something creative and easy. I took a course in hairstyling. The second challenge came as we moved to a whole new society. In 1975, Ricky was three years old. We moved to the United States. All of us came here in order to begin a new life in the land of freedom and opportunity. This is a beautiful country. It gives you the chance to learn and achieve whatever you set your mind on. The greatest gift our parents gave us as children was moving to the United States. We started our life in a totally different environment. It was a faster pace of life with different people.

The mentality was different. The country was a new country; everything was new. Now we had to adjust to the new lifestyle. It is much easier than living in a place where you have to answer everyone's questions, where you come from and where you are going to. They are constantly watching and judging you. It was a big break for me. It was actually turning the page from a conditioned culture to an open society. I started my life here with a renewed joy of living. I could now breathe easily without the pressure of judgment. For a long time, I had felt myself like a caged bird. Now the door has been opened, and I flew away. I flew to a different place, looking for more adventure, growth, knowledge, and life experiences. I loved my freedom! There was now freedom of thought, of speech, of action, of expression without concern about breaking any rules. For the first time in my life, I realized that everything happens for a purpose, good or bad. It does not matter. Whatever happens is for our own good and our own progress.

In the book of, *The Prophet* by Kahlil Gibran, the poet spoke of joy and sorrow:

> Your joy is your sorrow unmasked.
>
> And the selfsame well from which your laughter rises was oftentimes filled with your tears.
>
> And how else can it be?
>
> The deeper the sorrow carves into your being, the more joy you can contain.
>
> Is not the cup that holds your wine the very cup that was burned in the potter's oven?
>
> And is not the lute that soothes your spirit, the very wood that was hollowed with knives?
>
> When you are joyous, look deep into your heart and you shall find it is only that which has given you sorrow that is giving you joy.

When you are sorrowful look again in your heart
and you shall see that in truth you are weeping
for that which has been your delight.

How true is that. The moment we experience pain and sorrow, we think this is the end of the world. But the truth is that it is a process of purification and of growth toward a better understanding of life. It is a process of enlightenment, awareness, and consciousness.

The third challenge faced me as I began another marriage. The healing process went on slowly, but I was beginning to enjoy life day by day. One day after work, I stopped at my sister's house. We were reminiscing about our days in high school when her sister-in-law stopped by. After exchanging hi's and hello's, the conversation of marriage and meeting someone special came about. The lady mentioned that she knew a wonderful gentleman. He is a cousin of her husband. He lived in Ohio, and he was looking for a special person. For some reason, I enjoyed the conversation. I forgot that I had been hurt and was already divorced. I welcomed the idea, and again I took a chance at another relationship. I thought I was healed!

She carried on, talking about this gentleman and how wonderful he was. The thought that I might meet this individual became more attractive and more appealing to me. She asked if I would give her permission to invite him to visit us, and I did not object to the idea. I strongly believed that I would find my soul mate who will give me happiness, failing to realize that happiness is not given, happiness is found within.

I received a phone call telling me that the gentleman was in town and that he would like to meet me. I always kept in mind that I must conduct myself within the boundaries of balanced action that reflects high morals and standards with no consideration to either time or place. I asked him to meet me at my parents' house. By ten-thirty in the morning, he was over at my parents' house. He mostly concentrated in his talk on the future and the dreams of establishing a happy and successful life. As a first impression, I did not like the doubts and fears I had. I asked him if he was stable and successful in his life now or if he was expecting to be so in the future. He assured me that he was stable and successful in his business and lifestyle and is looking forward to a greater progress. The meeting ended by telling me that he would like to get to know me better and expressed his pleasure of meeting me again. I then proceeded with my daily life. This gentleman called me at least once a day. He was very aggressive and very determined to have me as a wife. Months of daily conversation, attention, recognition, and many words of love and compassion had their effect on me. I made up my mind that it was about time to go to the next step. Of course, that is a formal engagement.

A year and a half after the engagement, we got married. I left my family in Michigan and moved to Ohio together with my son Ricky and my husband. That started a new life for my son, and it was a great adjustment for both of us. We had to conform to his family, his business, his past relationships, and everything else. It was a new experience.

About three years into the marriage, I had another wonderful experience in life. Another guardian angel was born, and that was my daughter Valentina. She was my pride and joy. She was everything to me and to Ricky. Ricky was ecstatic, very happy and very proud of his sister. He cared for her, held her, and played with her. He was just there for her. The three of us had the nicest experience together. We were a very close family.

My husband was busy with his work. There were no lines of communication. The relationship was built on his success and his dreams. I started to realize what kind of man he was. I did not want to judge him, but the poor soul suffered from a great ego. Now I had two children and a relationship that was falling apart. I stayed with him for seven years. I did my share in the business, and I was a faithful wife, a true friend, and a true partner. He took everything for granted. Finally, I could not take it anymore, so I left him. I moved back to Michigan accompanied by my children. He followed us. He wanted me back, saying he loved me. He told me how wonderful I was, that I was the best. He vowed he would give me everything. He virtually promised me the moon. It made no sense to me anymore.

I was out, and I was not going back. It was over and done with. Now I had to deal with the death of another relationship, and again I had to struggle in life with full responsibility to my two children. I will make it because I believe in God and in myself. The most important thing I had is peace of mind. I also had harmony with myself and my children. I am proud of them, they are proud of me too, and I had to answer to no one. I was in a country where millions of people are divorced and no one asks why. My only concern was my two beautiful children and me. I knew the road was long and full of thorns, but I decided to make it. Some have truly said, "Where there is a will, there is a way." This realization did put me on the road of healing again, the road of healing and recovery.

Rabindranath Tagore says in his poem "My Friend,"

> I have come to thee to take thy touch before I begin
> my day.

> Let thy eyes rest upon my eyes for a while.

> Let me take to my work the assurance of thy
> comradeship, my friend.

Fill my mind with thy music to last through the
    desert of noise!

Let thy love's sunshine kiss the peaks of my thoughts,
    and linger in my life's valley where the harvest
    ripens.

Yes, indeed, the God within us is our strength. He will always guide us and rescue us from our difficulties and troubles and lead us to the safe shores, knowing that my strength and all answers come from within and that God's will is mine.

I believe that where there is a will, there is a way. I set my goal. First things first. I decided to take the path of education and knowledge. I went to college for two years and studied psychology. The subject gave me insight into human behavior and helped me deal with the limitations and insecurities resulting from frustrations and disappointments.

In June of 1985, we moved to Phoenix, Arizona, where my parents resided at that time. It was a good move because the weather was nicer and the sun always shines. Back east, the weather is gloomy most of the time. The sun does not smile. That kind of weather is depressing, but sunny Arizona is refreshing. It gave me hope and inspired me to do many things. I took nice walks in the evenings. I went to the zoo with my children. My parents asked us to live with them. It was convenient at the time because things were not good for me financially. As soon as I settled in, the first thing I did was to register in a college for interior design. I was very happy with this subject. I expressed myself through interior design. It was the way I wanted to be known. I made many friends in college. The children went to school, and we actually got used to the life in Arizona. We were happy with our new life.

Ricky was the first grandson in the family and was very special to my mother and father, especially to my mother. Ricky and Valentina became very attached to my parents. When we moved to Arizona, Ricky's age was thirteen and a half and Valentina's was five and a half.

Ricky's number one interest was to learn how to drive and one day have his own car. Who was the one who never rejected Ricky's requests? Of course, it was my mother.

She started giving him driving lessons and volunteered her time to teach him. She was a very cautious driver herself. Ricky loved every moment of it. When I saw how happy my children were, I felt good about the move I had made. I felt good to be back with my parents. It gave the children and me a sense of belonging. It was that assurance that I needed for myself and for my children. We really spent quality time together all around. It was just a great, great time.

II

January 21, 1987

For some reason, we were, on this day, extremely happy and cheerful. My mom was busy with baking some pastry. Ricky came home from school. He was too excited and happy. He shared with my mother and me a letter he received from a girl. The girl did not give her name or sign the letter. The next day, Ricky determined to find out who this lovely girl was who wrote him this love letter. I read the letter. It was a beautiful one. He was feeling so confident, happy, and proud. He was telling jokes to my mother and me.

During the conversation, he told my mother that he had a project to do for school and that he needed to go to the hardware store and pick up some wood and nails. My mom said she would go too so she could buy some things she needed. It was around four o'clock when my dad went with my mom to the car to wish her a safe trip and to drive carefully and that he would see them when they got back. Before he left, Ricky hugged me and kissed me and told me he loved me. He also kissed Valentina and said good-bye. Mom also said good-bye, and they left. Valentina, my dad, and I stayed behind because I had to do some homework. I went into the room, opened my books, and started doing my homework. Valentina had some coloring to do for a school project.

III

It was six o'clock, and my dad was watching TV while I was sitting in the bedroom doing my homework. I had a very uneasy feeling. I did not know how to explain it, but I was afraid of something. I did not want to share it with anyone. I kept it inside.

Then around six-thirty, my dad came to the bedroom and expressed his concern that mom and Ricky were late. I tried to reassure him that they would be home soon, but my uneasy feeling mounted and got stronger. It was eight o'clock, and they had not come back home yet. It was not like my mother's habit. If she said an hour and a half, it was an hour and a half, then she would be back.

Overwhelmed with deep sadness, I started panicking inside and got very nervous. My dad started getting nervous too. We looked out the window; then we went outside to the street. I guess we felt if we kept busy by walking, maybe they would show up. Then it was nine o'clock. They had not come back.

I suggested to my father that he drive his car and go look for them by taking the same route they took and I would stay home in case they called. My dad took off. He was so shaky and nervous. I had never seen him like this before.

As for me, I was ready to explode and scream. I cannot express or explain what I was feeling at the time. My heart was going a hundred miles an hour. I felt like it was going to stop. I felt something had happened, but I had no answer nor control over it. Neither one of us knew what was going on or what had happened to them. Valentina and I stayed behind.

I sat next to the telephone with my hand practically on the receiver. Forty-five minutes later, my dad came back. I met him outside. His face was white as a sheet. He looked at me and read the fears and doubt in my eyes. We both did not know what to say or what to do. I asked him if he saw them or found out anything about them. His voice turned shaky as he uttered that he had not seen anything at all. We went into the house. We sat close to the phone with our eyes fixed at the clock, and the minutes and the hours ticked away.

It was 10:30 p.m. I started to cry. I knew something horrible had taken place. There was not a shade of doubt in my mind. My father and I were overwhelmed with devastating emotions— pain, depression, sadness, helplessness, fear, and emptiness. We did not know what to do. We called the police and asked them if any accidents had taken place, but we got no answer to what we needed to know. We were both infuriated and flew into a rage and started yelling at each other, yet it was not anyone's fault. It was because we had no answers to any of our questions.

The last time my father and I looked at the clock was when it pointed to 11:00 p.m. A few minutes after eleven, the doorbell rang. My father and I ran to the door. We opened it, and there stood two policemen. They had the answers to what had happened. Their faces looked as though they had seen an apparition. I asked the policemen where my son and mother were. My dad asked them where his wife and grandson were. They tried to calm us down. They asked who Mr. Daniel is, and my dad introduced himself.

At this point, the policemen did not realize that I had asked them about my son. They asked my father if Luigina Daniel was his wife. They told him that she had his son or maybe his grandson with her and asked if he was around fourteen and a half years old. I told them that he was my son and asked them what had happened. They told me that they were sorry, but there had been an accident.

No sooner had they uttered that phrase that my father and I exchanged quick glances at each other, and both of us felt as though something deep inside us was extinguished. We did not know what to say. We both had tears in our eyes when we asked them if they were alive, and they told us they were at the morgue.

When I heard these words from the policemen, I felt the earth stopped turning, the sun perished, and the day and the night were put out of existence. It was the end of my life. I did not want to live. My dad and I broke down and cried. I wanted to attack these policemen. I wanted to hurt them because they hurt me by saying my mother and son were dead. I could not accept what I had heard. I did not believe the news they brought to us. My dad and I felt alone without any existence. We kept asking ourselves, "What now? What now?"

I told my dad that we were going to continue to wait. I was sure they will come back. I was crying. I was numb. I could not comprehend or believe what had taken place or what had happened. In the midst of my crying, I realized that my dad was talking to me. He was telling me that we should call the family and let them know what had happened.

My dad was stronger than me, or maybe he pretended to be strong at that moment in order to find out the details from the policemen.

My father called our family and relatives in Michigan, New York, Australia, Israel, and England. Everyone that my dad got in touch with was taken by surprise, stunned, and devastated. It was unbelievable what had happened. I would never forget that day for the rest of my life.

I could not sleep all night. I had to call Ricky's father in Israel to tell him the bad news. When I talked to him, he broke down and cried. The last time he saw Ricky was in August of 1986. Ricky visited his father in Israel as an adult for the first time since he was nine months old. It seemed like Ricky went there to bid his father adieu. It was the country where he was born. While I was telling him about our son's tragedy, I felt as though I was talking about strangers and not about my son and mother. I was both talking and crying. My dad took over the conversation because he noticed that I was distracted. I was crying and screaming and going totally out of control. My father became very worried about me. He told Ricky's dad that it would be good if he could come to the United States for the funeral. My father and I did not sleep that night.

Every morning Ricky's alarm clock goes off to wake him to go to school. That morning, Ricky was not in his bedroom. No light in the bathroom. No audible sound of his footsteps. The deadly silence dominated his bedroom. I could not accept the fact that Ricky and my mom were gone. I was in a state of total confusion and distraction.

In the background, I heard my daughter calling me. She just woke up and had no idea what had taken place last night.

She came to Ricky's bedroom looking for me and saw me crying. I looked like something from a horror movie. Even though she was only six years old, she knew when I was happy or sad. She knew something has gone wrong. She asked me why I was crying and why I was sad. What was I going to tell her? How was I going to explain it to her?

How was I going to make her understand that she would never ever see her brother or her grandmother again? I tried to explain to her as much as I can. I told her how much I loved her, but I had to tell her something very sad. I told her there was an accident and that Ricky and Grandma were killed. She reacted very quickly and angrily. She started crying, and she said she wanted Ricky and Grandma now.

I held her in my arms, and we both cried together. There is no explanation to a situation like that. There is no remedy for it. I took her back to the bedroom, and I sat with her and tried to explain, as much as possible, without falling apart myself, though I was already torn into pieces. With whatever was left of me, I tried to explain to my six-year-old daughter that her brother and her grandmother passed on with no justification. It happened so suddenly. They were happy. They were very healthy. They were there last night. Mother was cooking, Ricky was playing with Valentina, but then it just happened.

How are little children going to accept death when the only thing they know is life? A sudden change is beyond their comprehension. They always feel everything is all right. I tried to explain to Valentina that Ricky and Grandma are with the angels now. They are in a happy place. They are in a beautiful garden, and they are safe. It made no difference to her. She continued crying and calling their names. My dad came into the room and tried to calm her. Here I was with my six-year-old child trying to explain to her a situation that I myself could not accept or understand. I felt helpless, hopeless, and very much distressed.

There was no way to turn away from all this. This was something that I had to face and deal with. But how? How? I did not have the means. I did not have the understanding. I didn't have the patience. I was a mother who had lost her son and a daughter who lost her mother. I felt that by losing my mother, I became an orphan. By losing them both, I felt as though a great part of my life had perished. My dreams and hopes for my son's future, his talents, his love that I treasured—all has gone in a twinkle of an eye, and I no more wished to be.

My desire for survival pined. My son and I were put together and unified from birth. Nine months of anticipation. I watched him grow up slowly in front of my eyes. He was growing up to be a wonderful and great young man. Suddenly, he was taken away from me. All these dreams had vanished in a moment.

Abruptly, the phone rang while I was laden with grief and felt as though it was the end of the world for me. Life stopped its throbbing. I didn't want to talk to anyone. I didn't want to listen to anyone. I didn't want to see anyone. The phone kept ringing, so my dad answered the call. In the meantime, Valentina came back to me.

I sat her on my lap and clasped her arms. My father was talking to my sister, my two brothers, and other members of the family, arrived at the airport. They were all at the airport. They wanted us to know that they would arrive within half an hour. The half hour seemed to me like a year. The confusion and the nagging questions with no answers did not cease.

I wanted to see some familiar faces.

Perhaps they knew what had happened. Maybe they could answer the questions that I had been asking myself endlessly. The doorbell rang. My sister, my two brothers, my uncle and his wife, and other family members walked through the door. Everybody seemed stunned. They looked like they had not slept all night. There was so much pain in their faces. My sister and my brothers rushed on and hugged me. And soon, I fell apart, as had happened all along. There were not many words to be said, just crying. After a while, they tried to comfort me and lighten my pain. They talked to me and told me that Ricky and Mother are in a better place where peace and harmony dominated. That world is unlike this world, which is full of pain, worry, suffering, disappointment, disillusionment, and people killing one another. At least they are relieved from being inflicted with such agony, pain, and despair.

They tried to console me by telling me all these things, but they had no effect on me. At that moment, I did not want to even hear what they had to say because it would make no difference. Ricky was not around. My mom was not around! What difference did it make to say a few words munched by people's thought. No one was in my shoes.

Yes, my mother was their mother, but my son was mine; and I had to deal with a double tragedy. It was very difficult for anyone in this world to convince me that they were in a better place at that moment. My dad and my two brothers were talking about preparations for the funeral. They did not consult with me about anything. They took over and handled all details that were to take place the next day. In an instant, the house brimmed with people. It seems news travels fast, and the phone did not cease from ringing. Everyone called to pay their condolences, and many people were inquiring about the details of the funeral. So insensitive and ignorant, are they! Who has the heart to explain how they got killed or why? Heartless people.

Later on, the doorbell rang; and for some reason, I opened it. A young man, my son's age, stood at the door and asked if Ricky was at home. Right away, I said, "What do you mean is Ricky here? Don't you know? Ricky passed away!" Stunned, he replied, "Oh no! I did not know. I just came from California. I live there. I come to visit my grandparents in Phoenix every two weeks, and Ricky was my friend." Then I looked at the young man and said to him, "Please come in." Just knowing that he was a friend of my son made him a very special person to me. He stayed until eleven o'clock that evening, and all that time he sat next to me. His presence comforted me. He was telling me about his close friendship with Ricky and what he thought of him. I felt like holding this young man in my arms and not letting him go. I did not understand why I felt this way.

I just felt that if I just held on to this young man, I would be embracing my own son. This young man was the first of all Ricky's friends to come and ask about him. Isn't it ironic that this young man came all the way from California at this particular time when I very much needed support. This young man was there for me at the right time. It was just destined to happen that way.

IV

It was late. Everyone started leaving. The only people who stayed at home were my sister, my two brothers, my uncles and cousins from out of town. After everyone went to sleep, I went outside. The night was pitch-dark. No stars glimmered in the sky. I used to always go outside and look at the stars and the moon, but now it was so dark. It seemed like the stars and moon died too. I went into the house, took a shower, and put on my pajamas. Maybe I could get some rest. Who was I kidding? How could I sleep when my son and mom were not home yet? I was still waiting for their return.

The next morning, everyone started getting ready for the funeral. Whose funeral was it? What church? Then it dawned on me. It was for my son and my mother. I guess I have to get dressed. I put on a charade to look and act strong. How can I ever accept their sudden departure? What is it all about? Is there no one to explain to me what is going on here? Again the house was filled with people, and everyone was ready to go to the funeral. They were all waiting for me. I was just falling apart. "Everyone, just leave me alone!" What do these people want me to do? They want to force me to go bury my son and my mother. It is not up to them. This is my son and my mother. It is not their son and their mother. So why are they standing around waiting for me to get ready and dressed and to sit in the limousine and go to the church and then hand them over my son and my mother? Just pick them up and bury them! Is that what they wanted me to do? Why can't they understand what is happening to me? Why can't they feel my pain, my bereavement, and my aching heart.

My aunt came to me and explained in a very loving way that it had to be done. I had to accept the fact that they were gone, and there was no one or anything that could bring them back. She said, "It is a process that you have to go through, and God be with you, that is how it works." So I cried again until my eyes were inflamed, dried, and drained. My voice was practically gone. I got up and got dressed and sat in the limousine as it drove away, taking me to the church. I walked into the church, and my heart fell to my knees. I saw two coffins; my son's picture on one, and my mother's picture on the other. I went straight to Ricky's coffin and tried to open it. My two brothers came and held my arms and tried to talk to me, to calm me down. Their voices were breaking up from crying. I went to my mom's coffin and did the same. Kindly, they guided me to the front row to sit. Valentina was with me; and she saw all this devastation happening to me, and she fell apart. It was a very sad moment, and when the priest was praying and mentioning their names, everyone in the church broke down and cried. The church was filled with Ricky's friends. They loved my son very much. He was much loved by his teachers, his friends, and his acquaintances. He was very special to everyone who knew him or came in touch with him. I could not stop myself from crying. I felt so helpless because I could not see my son, I could not see my mom. I did not know who were in the coffins. All that I saw were the pictures of Ricky and my mother, and everybody told me that they had died.

Suddenly, I developed a hatred and resentment toward the priest, the owners of the funeral home, the people who arrayed the bodies and prepared the coffins, and all who were involved in these procedures. I instantly hated all of them. The priest continued to recite his prayers. In my eyes, it was just a mechanical and routine job. He did not feel or understand what I was going through. It was normal to him. He did that all the time

After he finished his job, everyone got up and waited outside. The next thing I knew was that all were in their cars. I was in the limousine, and we were on our way to the cemetery. I felt myself like a robot as though I had no will to do or to say anything. It was just like watching a movie. It was someone else's funeral, not my son's and my mother's. I went through the devastating emotions, knowing I would never see them again. Everyone was in a hurry to get rid of them. I was hoping that everyone would just disappear.

I could not believe what was taking place. The entire experience was that of disbelief and confusion. The priest was praying. He appealed to the Lord to have mercy on their souls. He was praying that they would enter the kingdom of heaven. I was experiencing hell. I screamed and cried. No matter what I did, I could not stop what was going on. The crying never stopped. I was in a totally different world, in a different state of mind. I was not myself. I was not in control. I could not control my feelings, and I was careless. I did not care at that moment what people thought of my behavior or my looks or my personality. I did not care about anything!

What was important to me was gone. There was nothing to live for anymore. It would be great if I died that very moment because I would be with them. I no longer cared to live.

Yet there was that little angel who kept me anchored to this life. It was my daughter. I had a beautiful little girl who counted on me.

She was going through her own personal pain. No one was paying her any attention because she was so young. They thought she did not understand what was going on, but Valentina really did know. She too had questions that needed answers.

V

I looked around me in the cemetery, and I could not believe my eyes at the multitude of people gathered there. Where did these people come from? Who were they? There were young adults, middle-agers, and old people. Evidently, all these people cared, and that is why they came here. At least in these moments, humanity showed love and care. After the priest ended all his prayers and the ceremony was completed, everyone started moving to his car. The family suggested that it was better for me to leave because I was in a hysterical mood. I did not see when they lowered the caskets. The family made a decision that it was safer for me not to see all of these procedures. As I was being driven away in the limousine, I saw many people, many cars, and the same two caskets. I cried and said, "Good-bye, Mom. Good-bye, Ricky," and the limousine drove away.

We got back to the house. All I wanted was to close the bedroom door and be all alone. I did not want interruptions or questions. I didn't want people to repeat to me the oft-repeated words. I did not want to eat or drink. I wanted to be in isolation and deal with this by myself. I wanted a moment to connect with my son and my mother spiritually. I needed them to talk to me, to give me a sign, to explain to me. I needed my mom to tell me how to handle the situation. I was so lost, so confused. None of these people—not even my father, my sister, my brothers, my uncle or aunt, or any of my relatives or friends—could give me answers that I was looking for. The only ones that could answer me were Ricky and my mother, and they were not talking to me.

They were not "communicating" with me. Only silence dominated deep in my heart. I was hoping and wishing that they would answer me. This was my third day with no sleep or rest. I was terribly exhausted. My health was deteriorating, and there was nothing I could do about it. The only time a person cares about his or her health is when he knows that he is going to be achieving, succeeding, or traveling. At such times, the person looks forward to being strong because the individual is expecting a wonderful life. As for me, I had just lost the most precious part of my life. I needed my space to deal with this devastating loss. My mind had not yet accepted the fact that Ricky and my mom were gone.

All the guests prepared themselves to leave and go home. My sister and brothers stayed for two extra days, and it was just the same for me as well as for them. My two brothers and my father still had to find a lawyer to represent us against the railroad company. I could not be present because I was not in a normal state of mind. They took care of it and appointed a lawyer. The sad thing was that lawyers only think of money. This situation was more than about money. It was about a family. In the eyes of the law, I would be suing the railroad company and also my mother's estate. This was because she allowed my son to drive the car. My father was suing the railroad because of the death of my mother and my son. My father had to defend my mom's estate against my suing them. It was a very complicated and sad situation. I did not want anything to do with all that. What is money compared to a human life? But then, that is how the law works. I let my brothers and my father take care of it the best they could.

I wanted to stay out of it until I could deal with the situation. I was grieving. Money meant nothing to me. It would be so tomorrow and forever because money would never bring back the two people I love. After the funeral, I realized my two brothers and dad would leave for at least a couple of hours every day. They would go to the police station to discuss matters. Everybody kept me in the dark about what was going on. Later on, I understood that the police wanted my father and two brothers to go back to the accident scene. This they did.

My father told me the reason later. Mom's car had stalled on the railroad tracks. The train hit the car at 80 mph, causing the car to turn over on its side. Ricky's body ejected out from the window of the car. The train pushed the car more than one mile. My son's body got caught in the wheels of the train. Half of his body was found in the last car of the very long train. That particular train was the longest passing train through that area on that day. The police called my father and two brothers to go back to the site of the accident to collect the remains of the skin and bones of my son's body. They took the remains to church for proper burial arrangements. All this took place without my knowledge.

There was another thing I found out. Ricky's coffin was closed because his body was in a bag, and there was not much left to see. My brothers and my father saw my mom. It was now confirmed by them that she really had died. Such information were conveyed to me many months later. I kept asking. I wanted to know, and I wanted to see and understand.

They kept withholding all that they knew and tried always to change the subject. They made all kinds of excuses. My father and my two brothers saw the scene of the accident. They saw it in details, but never told me anything about it.

The fifth day after the tragedy, my two brothers and my sister had to leave back to their families and business. So, I was home with only my father and my daughter. But yet people desisted not from coming over to pay their condolences. Others called and some others sent sympathy cards. Unfortunately, that never cured my pain nor brought my beloved ones back to me. I had to deal with this actuality day in and day out, without sleeping or eating. I lost much of my weight. I ended up weighing 90 pounds.

As far as Valentina was concerned, I developed fears and doubts, so I did not allow her to go back to school. I much needed her to be with me, and make sure she is safe. I much needed her every other moment of the day. I needed her at home. I called her school and told the person in charge about the situation. I could not handle anything to do with vehicles nor can I bear to keep my daughter away from me.

One day, my sister called and suggested that my father, Valentina and I go to Michigan for a change I discussed the matter with my father, He said it would be a good idea. We agreed to leave for Michigan at the end of February. In the meantime, my father and I turned like water mixed with oil. We had arguments and disagreements. I just wanted to yell at him. I took all my anger out on him and he did the same to me. We could not see an eye to eye on anything. Both of us lost loved ones and both of us were much hurt, frustrated and our life turned sad and miserable. We were grieving and found no answers to our questions. Both of us were asking the same questions.

VI

Despair took over our reasoning. "Why did it happen? How are we to deal with the situation?"

My father and I ignored each other. I was angry and disrespectful toward him. It was beyond my will. I love him. He is a wonderful and beautiful soul. But at that moment, at that time, I could not see the wonderful soul that he had. I saw a person with whom I wanted to start a fight with for no real reason. It was just because he had no answers for me. Why did that have to happen to me? Why were we not there for them? Though we could not save them! We both felt guilty, so guilty that we wanted to explode. A great deal of anger took over, and it took the peace of mind that I had once.

The time when my children and I began to feel comfortable, the tragic event took place. It destroyed our hopes, our dreams, the harmony and the security that we all felt. I had to deal with it by myself. What about Ricky's father? He could not attend the funeral. The only time we spoke was when I phoned him and told him of the dreadful news. I was angry about that also. I handled the situation by myself. I carried the burden alone, and that escalated both my anger and frustration. At least when the parents are there, the situation eases off as they can help each other and cope with the matter in a better way. So who was there to support my broken heart and my life that had fallen apart? Of course, my little six-year-old, Valentina. When she used to see me crying, she would come and sit next to me and tell me how much she loved me and that she wanted to take care of me.

She played the mother role, and I felt so good and relaxed knowing there was one who shared with me my feeling. At that time, my daughter did a better job than my father.

Under all circumstances, he too needed someone to listen to him and to console him, and I was not there for him. In my eyes, Valentina became both my daughter and my son. She automatically took the place of Ricky. I saw Ricky in Valentina's person by the way she talked, the way she thought, the way she supported me. She was exactly like Ricky when he was at her age. And that was a big comfort to me. It was as though a part of Ricky was still alive. It gave me hope. It gave me something to cling to and hold on to. Valentina became very precious, much more than ever before.

Being alone together, it was a little calmer. There were fewer phone calls and fewer people coming around. I started to go into Ricky's bedroom, looking for his personal things, things that meant a lot to him. I saved them. I looked at his hairbrush, and I found some hair in it, Ricky's hair. I took it and put it in a plastic bag, and I still have it.

I asked my father to take me to see the car they drove. He took me to the wreckage yard. No sooner had my eyes caught sight of the car and its condition that I fell apart and started crying. My god, for sure, they could not survive. It was like taking a piece of paper and crumbling it in your hands. That was the shape of the car. I looked inside it and saw his shoes. I was so lucky to have found them. I took the shoes and then saw a white sheet that my mom used as a seat cover on the driver's seat. The sheet was full of blood.

It was the blood of my son and my mother. I still have the sheet and Ricky's shoes. I sent the shoes to a workshop in Ohio and had them gold-plated.

On the first week of February 1987, the police called my dad to go to the police station. When my dad got there, they gave him Ricky's wallet. When they changed my mom's clothes and put on her good clothes, they gave what she was wearing on that tragic day to my father. To this day, I have them. I cannot part with them. I feel close to these things because they are the clothes and possessions of the awful unforgettable accident.

The second week of February, a lady friend of the family called and tried to tell me that I needed to join a support group that would help in dealing with my loss. I asked her for the phone number, as I did not want to turn her down. But I never went to a support group. I never talked to anybody. I did not have any counseling. I did not see a psychiatrist or even a doctor. I did not take any medicine. I preferred to face this ordeal by myself. It happened to me suddenly and I had to deal with it delicately. I was sure that God within me would give me the strength to find my way and see the light to deal with the unexpected horrible situation that I was in.

I dealt with my grief and loss one step at a time. I went at my own speed. I did not need to be rushed. I did not want a psychiatrist or a psychologist to feed me snatches of advices such as to be strong, accept the fact that my beloved ones are gone, and all the sadness was not going to bring them back to me. I did not want to hear all this. I wanted to feel everything as is, to deal with it and face it by myself.

I did not need anyone to push me to heal, for I believed I would heal in my own way, slowly but surely. I needed to digest the idea, the feeling, and the thought of what happened. I had to accept that they were safe in a different place. I had to learn to heal myself in solitary confinement. I needed God to have mercy upon me and help me. I did not need any other human being to help me because he has nothing to say except these few words: "forget" and "let go" and "start all over again." I did not want to let go, I did not want to start all over again, and I did not want to forget. I know my son is physically gone, but spiritually he lives within me and around me. I did not need anyone to convince me to forget or to let go because there was nothing to forget or let go of.

On the third week of February, we started packing and preparing ourselves to leave for Michigan. My life didn't change. I was still crying every night, still not eating or sleeping well, for I was absorbed in thinking of the cycle of events. Still there were no answers or solutions. The end of February had come, and we were ready to fly to Michigan. My sister and my two brothers met us at the airport with tears and deep sorrow. My sister tried to cheer me up by telling me, "It is good that you came here. We will go to many places and do things together." "Thank you, thank you, dear sister," I replied.

The weather was very cold. It was still winter, and my immune system was weak. I caught a cold. It went into my lungs, causing me to become very ill with pneumonia. I was coughing all the time while I was in Michigan. I was sick for almost three months, and that reduced my appetite for eating, and I became weaker than before. I was still grieving and crying.

My sister and brothers organized a memorial mass with the church. I could not go to the memorial. I could not bear any memento of what had happened. Everyone, including friends and family, asked about me. They came to see me. I told my sister, "I do not want to see anybody. Please try to understand." I stayed in my bedroom all day and all night. I became a hermit; I just did not feel any need to answer any question that I did not know the answer to. How could I answer these questions? I only wanted to be left alone. I appreciated their effort and their care. It was more of curiosity than anything else on their part. Staying away from everybody gave me a peace of mind. I needed tranquility and peacefulness that would enable me to cope with the situation. I needed to find solutions and answers to questions that no one could answer except the higher self and God's divine mind.

VII

My healing started by acknowledging the loss. I struggled between both belief and disbelief. It happened, and it was real. I knew that God within me was the source of my strength. I knew I was still alive. That meant that I was strong and would survive. There was nothing I could change. It happened. Yes, I did feel angry, outraged, and melancholic. I felt numbed and frightened. All these feelings were because I am human. I know loss is part of life itself. And loss is a test for human courage. Part of the healing process and growth was the feeling I went through that wavered. One day I felt I am okay, the next day I felt I would hit the bottom. It seemed as though it would go on forever. One thing I did that helped me heal was to read all kinds of metaphysical books. I read about meditation, yoga, and higher consciousness. I learned how to breathe. By breathing, I realized I was alive. I learned through meditation how to commune with God. It did help me very much. I felt at peace with myself when I realized there is no separation between us. Ricky, my mom, and I read *The Prophet* by Kahlil

Gibran more than once. The writing had insight on matters of love, religion, friendship, marriage, teaching, knowledge, pain, reason, passion, freedom, law, crime, and punishment.

The passage that I read more than once was about death. That was the main thing that helped me concerning some of the answers I was seeking. Gibran says,

> You would know the secret of death.
>
> But how shall you find it unless you seek it in the heart of life?
>
> The owl whose night-bound eyes are blind unto the day cannot unveil the mystery of light.
>
> If you would indeed behold the spirit of death, open your heart wide unto the body of life.
>
> For life and death are one, even as the river and the sea are one.

Here is another section about death:

> In the depth of your hopes and desires lies your silent knowledge of the beyond;

And like seeds dreaming beneath the snow your heart dreams of spring.

Trust the dreams, for in them is hidden the gate to eternity.

And this one is also about death:

Your fear of death is but the trembling of the shepherd when he stands before the king whose hand is to be laid upon him in honor.

Is the shepherd not joyful beneath his trembling, that he shall wear the mark of the king?

Yet he is not more mindful of his trembling?

I like this one:

Only when you drink from the river of silence shall you indeed sing.

And when you have reached the mountain top, then you shall begin to climb.

And when the earth shall claim your limbs, then shall you truly dance.

And about good and evil, Gibran wrote,

You are good when you strive to give of yourself.

Yet you are not evil when you seek gain for yourself.

For when you strive for gain you are but a root that clings to the earth and sucks at her breast.

Surely the fruit cannot say to the root, "Be like me, ripe and full and ever giving of your abundance."

For to the fruit giving is a need, as receiving is a need to the root.

And about joy and sorrow, he says,

Some of you say, "Joy is greater than sorrow," and others say, "Nay, sorrow is greater." But I say unto you, they are inseparable.

Together they come, and when one sits alone with you at your board, remember that the other is asleep upon your bed.

And about children, he wrote,

You may give them your love but not your thoughts,

For they have their own thoughts.

You may house their bodies but not their souls,

For their souls dwell in the house of tomorrow, which you cannot visit, not even in your dreams.

You may strive to be like them, but seek not to make them like you.

For life goes not backward nor tarries with yesterday.

You are the bows from which your children as living arrows are sent forth.

The archer sees the mark upon the path of the infinite, and he bends you with his might that his arrows may go swift and far.

Let your bending in the archer's hand be for gladness;

For even as he loves the arrow that flies, so he loves also the bow that is stable.

And about pain, he says,

Your pain is the breaking of the shell that encloses your understanding.

Even as the stone of the truth must break, that its heart may stand in the sun, so must you know pain.

And could you keep your heart in wonder at the daily miracles of your life, your pain would not seem less wondrous than your joy.

And you would accept the seasons of your heart, even as you have always accepted the seasons that pass over your fields.

And you would watch with serenity through the winters of your grief.

Much of your pain is self-chosen.

It is the bitter potion by the physician within you heals your sick self.

Therefore trust the physician, and drink his remedy
  in silence and tranquility;

For his hand, though heavy and hard, is guided by
  the tender hand of the Unseen,

And the cup he brings, though it burns your lips,
  has been fashioned of the clay which the Potter
  had moistened with His own sacred tears.

Another book that filled my soul with peace was the
collection of poems and plays of Tagore. One of his poems
ran as follows:

Let me not pray to be sheltered from dangers but
  to be fearless in facing them.

Let me not beg for the stilling of my pain but for
  the heart to conquer it.

Let me not look for allies in life's battlefield, but to
  my own strength.

Let me not crave in anxious fear to be saved but hope for the patience to win my freedom.

Grant me that I may not be a coward, feeling your mercy in my success alone; but let me find the grasp of your hand in my failure.

VIII

Some other books helped me and gave me strength. They helped me to answer questions I could not answer before. I read many spiritual books. I needed to go into a higher consciousness and resolve my confusion and misunderstanding about life and death. The spiritual books gave me insights and answers to what I was going through. They became my best friend. I did not want people to be around me, to talk to me, to comfort me, or to make me feel less devastated. The only friends I counted on were my books. The knowledge in the books taught me how to deal with my sorrow, sadness, and grief. They taught me how to look at what happened in a different way and how to approach my fears and doubts. They answered the questions of why it happened to me, what concerned about my son's dreams, and why did my loved ones leave without a warning? I had constantly faced these haunting questions in the past few months.

Carol Staudacher said in her book *Beyond Grief,*

> The death of a child is perhaps the ultimate shock, one which seems too horrendous to fathom. As you try to cope with what has happened, one of the most disturbing issues to deal with is the wrongness of your child's death. Because the natural order is for you to precede your child in death. You must, when your child dies, readjust to a new and seemingly illogical reality. This reality says that even though you are older, have been the caretaker, and have a shorter future, you have survived while your child, who had the right to survive, has not.
>
> This unique individual you loved so deeply has been taken away from you. Nothing nor no one can remedy your loss. Having other children or being able to have another baby does not diminish your grief over your child's death. Researchers have found, for example, that mothers who lose one baby in a set of twins grieve just as much as mothers who lose a single newborn baby . . . .
>
> In addition to coping with the loss of a particular and unique individual, you are also being seriously

affected by the absence of what your child represented to you.

He or she represented several, or even all, of the following:

- Part of yourself; part of your physical body.

- Your own connection to the future.

- Your love source.

- Some of your treasured qualities and talents.

- Your missed expectations.

- A loss of your own power.

In Elaine Vail's book *A Personal Guide to Living with Loss*, she wrote,

> Death has many different faces and yet just one. We perceive death in a certain way because of our particular experiences with death, our religious background, our philosophy of life, education, and even our "lot in life." Those who have an easy, comfortable life are more likely to view death as an evil than those who are enslaved and

abused, who may see death as a blissful release. How we deal with death depends on all of these factors, on our personality, and the presence of supporting, helpful people.

Death is universal. We know that each of us will die. Yet each death has a meaning of its own and a unique influence on others. How we perceive death is probably a crucial factor in the way we live our lives. Indeed, many authors have pointed out that only because our lives are finite do they have meaning. Many times, individuals have been spurred by the death of another into a significant discovery or great accomplishment. We feel an urgency to do all we can, love all we can, "grab all the gusto" because we don't have forever. It is unfortunate that it often takes a tragedy, an untimely death to make us realize the truth of our mortality. If we all died only at a ripe old age, probably only a few of us would truly appreciate our lives and make the most of our potential. Perhaps what seems to us as senseless, violent, or early deaths are sometimes God's message to the survivors to make the most of our lives now.

We face many crises in our lives. They are all losses of some measure. We lose jobs, get divorced, move away from home, fail tests, burn our breakfast toast, and miss the bus. Learning to cope with these crises is necessary and desirable. Otherwise we would be crippled, helpless, unable to function in an environment beset with imperfections, not the least of which are often our own. Each time we suffer one of these losses and somehow adapt to it, learn from it, and grow from it, we gain some skills, some insight, and some confidence in our own ability to survive such events.

Melba Colgrove says in her book *How to Survive the Loss of a Love*,

Don't postpone, deny, cover or run from your pain. Be with it. Now. Everything else can wait. An emotional wound requires the same priority treatment as a physical wound. Set time aside to mourn. The sooner you allow yourself to be with your pain, the sooner it will pass. The only way out is through. When you resist mourning, you interfere with the body's natural stages of recovery. If you postpone the healing process, grief can return months—even years—later to haunt you. Feel the fear, pain, desolation, anger. It's essential to the healing process. You are alive. You will survive.

These wonderful books taught me how to look at this situation with a very conscious mind. I learned how to commune with God by the help of Paramahansa Yogananda's book *How You Can Talk to God.*

Talking with God is a definite fact. In India I have been in the presence of saints while they were talking with the Heavenly Father. And all of you, also, may communicate with Him; not a one-sided conversation, but a real talk wherein you speak to God and He responds. Everyone can talk to the Lord, of course. But I am discussing today how we may persuade Him to reply to us.

Why should we doubt? The scriptures of the world abound in descriptions of talks between God and man. One of the most beautiful of these incidents is recorded in I Kings 3:5-13 (Holy Bible):

The Lord appeared to Solomon in a dream by 'night; and God said, Ask what I shall give thee. And Solomon said . . . Give therefore thy servant an understanding heart . . . And God said unto him, Because thou hast asked this thing, and hast not asked for thyself long life; neither hast asked riches for thyself, nor hast asked the life of thine enemies; but hast asked for thyself understanding to discern judgment; Behold, I have done according to thy words: lo, I have given thee a wise and an understanding heart . . . And I have also given thee that which thou hast not asked, both riches and honor.

I had the opportunity to find out who I was to my son and my mother and what my job and purpose in this lifetime are. Nature and solitude became part of my daily life. I needed to stand on my own two feet. I needed to face reality. I brought the power from within to the outside to deal with the situation. Slowly, one day at a time, I started to look into the purpose of their deaths, and I found it was for my own spiritual growth. It took me many months and many years to accept this fact. Reading hundreds of books made me understand and realize that I have nothing to fear. The God within me gave me strength to face the tragedy inflicted on me.

I needed to start the search from beginning to end. The first thing I did was to search for the significance of metaphysics and its meaning. I found that it was the door to the unknown. It opened the door to the world for all answers. That is the source (God), the Cosmic Power. I started to slowly understand and grasp what all these wonderful authors offered.

They shared their writings, experiences, and their love to humanity. That is wonderful because they came to my rescue without even speaking a word (my eyes were to read and my mind to comprehend and digest).

In Shakti Gawain's book *Creative Visualization*, she writes,

> Let us imagine that life is a river. Most people are clinging to the bank, afraid to let go and risk being carried along by the current of the river. At a certain point, each person must be willing to simply let go, and trust the river to carry him or her along safely. At this point he learns to "go with the flow" and it feels wonderful.

> Once he has gotten used to being in the flow of the river, he can begin to look ahead and guide his own course onward, deciding where the course looks best, steering his way around boulders and snags, and choosing which of the many channels and branches of the river he prefers to follow, all the while still "going with the flow."

> This analogy shows us how we can be enjoying our here and now, flowing with what is, and at the same time be guiding ourselves consciously toward our goals by taking responsibility for creating our own lives.

Remember, too, that creative visualization is a tool that can be used for any purpose, including one's own growth in consciousness, it is often very helpful to use creative visualization in picturing yourself as a more relaxed, open person, flowing, living in the here and now, and always connected with your inner essence.

The more I read, the more I wanted to know.

All these books came at a perfect time. How great is God. All the answers came from within. These books brought me enlightenment. I realized how fortunate I was to experience everything on the face of this earth: the good and the bad. All of these experiences were a factor in my spiritual growth, and I learned how to rise above the petty problems that one's ego cannot solve. I give greatness and thanks to God for all I have experienced in this lifetime. I'd like to refer the reader to the concise treatise I have written on this subject (appearing at the end of this book).

IX

Ever since man was created, he has never ceased searching for a goal in his life. He sensed innately that his short stay on this earth was tasteless unless engrossed by a noble goal.

His creative imagination and visualization led him to believe in a power far stronger than his own bodily strength. Being so primitive, he invented several gods to worship, accessible gods that man can see, such as the sun, the moon, etc. Gradually, and much too late, he was convinced that what he used to worship in those ancient times were mere illusions and far from reality. He realized, through his thorough and incessant search, the following:

a. Nothing is created from nothing.

b. Man is created by the universal mind, and man's mind is but part of that universal mind. And this mind is able to set in motion a creative power, but such power is limited to his individuality and is capable to change causality in believing and desiring all that is only tuning with the cosmos, that is supposed to be always good.

It is a power hidden within man's own self that can produce all that is good and tunable with oneself and with the universe. It can produce happiness, peace, success, and all that is beneficial and constructive. It is equally true that this same power can produce out of fear and miserable forces such as sadness, failure, and all other types of negativity. "Both heaven and hell lie within each of us."

The individual power arises from our

1. Self-knowing, emerging from our self-consciousness

2. It gives us the freedom and the right to be self-choosing

Man is an individualistic entity, but God is the universal. Holmes writes, "For as the Father has life in Himself, so had He given to the Son to have live in Himself." He added, "God governs not through physical law as result, but first by Inner Knowing, then physical follows."

In just the same way, man governs his world. He governs it by the process that we call the "thought power," and man's mind activity is the "thought," and God is the "intelligence" who has no beginning or end. Man has, therefore, the same nature of

God in that he was given the freedom and the choice. He has an individual mind, and this mind is capable of thinking, of being aware and self-conscious. Man lives "in mind," and all thoughts brought to this mind are but a recurrence and reflection of his own lived life. That is why the common people thought that Jesus must be God. As Holmes says, "Because Jesus did understand and did use the great laws with objective consciousness, people thought He must be God."

Jesus was only God's manifestation, like all other human creatures who are of his creation.

"I say that ye are Gods, and every one of you, sons of the most high." Creation is done through mental law, then physically manifested. Accordingly, man is a creative power in his own right.

He has the full freedom to do what he likes, but this freedom is bound by the law and cannot operate outside of it. That is, his freedom stems from his full understanding of his own life's laws and compliance with them. This law is, in fact, God's law and God's spirit, whose impulse is the "unconditional love," and this law is always mental."

Holmes again says, "And so far as his thought goes, there is something that goes with it that has the power to bring forth into manifestation the thing thought of."

Hoffman in his writings of the Huna says, "When you finally realize you are the cause of everything in your life, you begin to know that as the cause, you can create what you want. You can control the events that happen to you because you are responsible for creating the context within which they occur."

The Maharishi attributes the belonging of this freedom to "the field of being." This field of being is established by practicing meditation, where man discovers his true inner self: "light" and "love."

The beginner should not be discouraged when he fails to achieve quick results. But through his perseverance and strong will, the tip of the balance will be in his favor.

a. He will pluck the fruit of his work and find that his body becomes more responsive to his spiritual will. He can thus deal with problems in a milder and more comprehensible way because his decision is based on quiet thinking. It has been proven that the thinking process starts from the most refined level of consciousness. The more it develops, the more its scope is opened to a wider understanding.

b. Due to the flow of energy, he will feel that he is more energetic. This brings him into harmony with both his spiritual and materialistic life. The mind is always capable of selecting what is useful of the coming thoughts and others that should be rejected.

c. His etheric body will be refined. It becomes a temple of peace, joy and health.

Shah, in his book *The Meditators*, says, "The Eastern religions have come up with an ideal antidote to this strong and unpopular teaching. There is that spark of divinity-that little piece of God in each one of us-that, if we can only get in touch with it through meditation, we can raise the level of our consciousness until we commune with the Cosmic Consciousness."

It is the same light that filled the room of Jacob Boehme, the German cobbler; the same light that shone upon Kabir, the Indian weaver; and it is the same light that blinded Paul for three days on his way to Damascus. It is the same light that lighted the cave of the prophet Mohammed. It is the same light that guided Albert Schweitzer to serve humanity in Gabon at the jungle village of Lambarene. It is the same light that guided the late Danny Thomas, the famous actor, to establish St. Jude Children's Research Hospital, which is considered the sixth largest charity institute in the United States.

"The dream that awakes the world." It is also the same light whose illumined flame will ever shine and show to all aspirants the way of truth. The only door to which a talk with the universal God is possible and where a transformation into a renewed soul is accomplished: "Thou wilt keep him in perfect peace whose mind is stayed on thee" (Isaiah 26:3).

This attained light is the full awareness with which a person may be blessed. It is the higher consciousness that some call the "third eye." All things come to the aspirant as a source of joy. It is the inner sense, the extra sensory perception (ESP), the "inner intelligence." It is its integration with the essence of this universe in all aspects. In attaining this stage, the aspirant realizes that all outside influences are in vain. They will disappear and be convert into positive elements. The more an aspirant develops this sense, the more his life will be filled with joy and peace. He is freed from all foreign material that may distract him. His nature is to be loved and strengthened. Without being free, happiness cannot be achieved. When one is freed from his worries, his fears, and all other negativity, he is totally free. When the majority is freed, the atmosphere and/or the environment reflects this bliss of freedom, and a healthy society emerges. Meditation is the way of life. It is the purifier of man's body and mind and a healer of "sins."

I shall leave physicians, physiologists, and psychologists to explain the scientific role that meditation plays in healing many of man's diseases and illnesses. Here below are some of the illnesses that might be cured through practicing meditation:

a. It lowers the blood pressure and slows down the pulse movement.

b. It keeps the meditator fresh and young.

c. It improves his emotional life.

d. It alleviates sexual dysfunction.

e. It regulates eating disorders and other similar ones.

f. It lessens heart attack.

g. It alleviates depression.

h. It curbs high cholesterol.

Let us keep practicing meditation and preserve it as one of our highest goals in life, for it is a way of living.

X

Looking out the window of my sister's family room—her children in school, my brother-in-law at work, my sister shopping—Valentina and I were home alone. The house was very peaceful. For the first time since I came to Michigan, I sat and watched the falling of snow. I realized the pond was frozen and the fourteen acres of maple trees were bare and the pure white snow covers the ground. What a cold and bare sight! It reminded me of myself. I felt devoid, numb, and frozen. I saw something approaching from behind the trees. A deer and her fawn came looking for some grass to eat. That was a very touching sight. Suddenly, I realized that just because it was cold and the snow covered everything and the grass is scarce does not mean the deer and her fawn would starve to death. Their minds were set on survival. Winter or summer, it did not matter. These are animals, but they knew how to survive (it is the intelligence that we are all part of God).

Then I took a look at my situation and said to myself, "Ricky and mom would not want me to die. They want me to continue to live and help others in the same situation, to help them cope with their loss." So once more, God is great to have given me this opportunity to experience these beautiful creatures and learn how to survive in the rain or sunshine. I shared this with my baby. She looked at the deer and her fawn and said to me, "Oh, Mom, it is like you and me, always together." I held her in my arms and told her how much I loved her. That sight gave me a chance to take a look at where I was going. The first thought that came to my mind was to prepare to go back to Phoenix.

So in May, I returned to Phoenix. The first thing I did was to look for my own house; I moved out of my father's house. It was just Valentina and I by ourselves. I could not afford a huge house, so I moved into a double-wide trailer. It was my first house without a husband. There was only my daughter and me. I needed the time to heal and I needed my solitude. I needed time to think and to find answers and solutions to my future and my daughter's. I was sure I made a very wise decision.

One thing had bothered me the entire time I was lying down in my new house. There was a railroad track four miles away from where the house was located and the trains were to pass from two o'clock until seven o'clock in the morning. As they did, they were to blow the horn. I could not rest remembering that my son and mother were killed by a train. What a memory and what a reminder; it was an everyday reminder. I was still dealing with grief. I asked for guidance in order to understand this mystery. I found an answer in Shakti Gawan's book, "Creative Visualization":

"In learning to use creative visualization, you may get in touch with blocks in yourself that hold you back from attaining your highest good."

A "block" is a place where energy is constricted—not moving, not flowing. Usually, blocks are caused initially by repressed emotions of fear, guilt, and/or resentment (anger) which cause a person to tighten up and close down spiritually, emotionally, mentally, and even physically.

In dealing with a block on any level, what's needed is to get energy moving and flowing in that area. The keys to this are the following:

1. Mental and emotional acceptance (on a physical level, this manifests as relaxation and release)

2. Clear observation, leading to understanding of the root of the problem, which is always a limiting attitude or belief

So in dealing with an area of consciousness where we have a block, we need to first experience (as fully as possible) the emotion we have locked up in that area in a loving, accepting way. In doing so, we get the blocked-up energy moving, and we have a chance to observe the underlying negative beliefs or attitudes that caused the problem to begin with. We can take a good, clear look at them and let them dissolve themselves.

I said to myself, *The train passing by every morning is not letting me sleep. It is because Ricky and my mother are saying hello to me every morning. They are saying, "We love you. We are happy. Do not be sad. You will find out in future that what had happened to us is for your own good."* That is an answer that came from within.

I had another insight. It was that I should get more education. So I went to college and registered for classes in interior design. That profession is very artistic and creative. It brought beauty from inside to the outside. I graduated with honors. I worked and produced money for myself and my daughter.

I still felt a yearning for more knowledge, so again I went to school and studied real estate, and that is when I met my wonderful better half, my husband Robert. I guess it was meant for us to meet each other. It was a wonderful experience. We went through hardships, struggles, concessions, and compromises. So we grew together into more conscious beings.

Robert had to learn to adjust to the loss of my son and my mother because it kept living within me. I did not become an expert on death and loss. I was moving one inch a day, and I am still moving one inch a day. But compared to where I was in the beginning, today I already crossed thousands of miles. That was due to the understanding I gained from reading these special spiritual, metaphysical, and the positive visualization books that turn the negative process into a positive one. My wonderful husband learned how to deal with my mood swings, the changes, the sudden sadness, the lack of appetite, and the lack of sleep. He learned to cope with my waking up crying in the middle of the night. He was there for me, and he was marvelous about it. He was and is my best friend.

He is also Valentina's friend and father. She chose that he would be her father because unfortunately, her paternal father was wrapped up in his ego, and he did not want to have any responsibility toward her, either financially or emotionally. Valentina had to make a decision. She and her father Robert love and respect each other. He admires and adores her, and she adores, loves, and respects him. We are a very blessed family to have one another. There was one thing that kept bothering me, my perpetual grieving.

It kept on and on. I have done so much on reading. It has shown me that though the bodies of my son and mother are gone, their spirits are always around us. There is no separation. Death does not separate the spirit. It only separates the physical form or core.

Joel S. Goldsmith, in his book *Collected Essays*, explains "Ye are the light":

> This *I am* is the universal Being, your Christ-Self; your true identity, the only one you have. We speak of "your" life, "my" life, or "his" or "her" life, whereas it is necessary for us to remember that there is in all the world only *one* Life. This Life is deathless, ageless, disease-less and changeless; it is the individual expression of that *one* divine Life. In other words, divine Life is our life. It contains no element of matter or discord, it curbs decomposition and holds fast decrepitude. This Life, of ours, is composed of spirit's core. It is infinite, eternal and harmonious. (emphasis added)

XI

Through healing the physical bodies, Christ symbolized a deeper healing at the existential level of the self. Man's greatest enemy is the "self"; it separates man from his wholeness and totality. When man's mind is dormant, the self is awake, and yet it is blindfolded. It lacks wisdom, love, and integrity with the unity of the universe. It is tuneless to all others. It is numbed to the state of consciousness. It is not in a position to hear the vibrations that usually come from consciousness's layers. It is totally detached from humanity, believing that its security stems from its amassing of powers, worldly material things, and what it believes to be successes, and yet whatever the self may levy, it still remains hungry and unsatisfied.

This low self is alleviated by growing. In growth, man starts to know himself and becomes well informed and more knowledgeable. This knowledge is the voice of the conscience. In this connection, Sechrist writes in her book *Meditation*,

"Conscience, the still small voice is the voice of the Divine within us, guiding our feet back to the path. Meditation is the way to greater awareness of the Divine." When this voice starts to speak in the mind, opening the way to your consciousness, then pain dissolves."

In *The Prophet*, Gibran says,

> Your pain is the breaking of the shell that encloses your understanding.

> Even as the stone of the fruit must break, that its heart may stand in the sun, so must you know pain.

> And could you keep your heart in wonder at the daily miracles of your life, your pain would not seem less wondrous than your joy;

Despite the great achievements made by man in different fields of civilization, he lives in a turbulent sea of fears and worries. These are his shackles, and all his attachments are but material ones. They are his "illusions," the fake and the unreal things. Only through breaking of the "shell" is he awakened. He then can realize what *I am* really means, that man is an idea that is eternal and infinite, and it was never born and will never die. The body in itself is nonactive; it only responds to the stimulus of the mind, and the source of all actions is the mind, the conscious.

Realizing these facts brings forth peace, joy, and harmony. God becomes visible, and this is the real goal that every person is seeking to attain.

XII

All the information I had been gathering and studying was wonderful, but still I wanted much more out of life. So one day, Valentina, my husband, and I decided to go to California. By chance, I was introduced to the publisher of *Al Wasat Al Arabi* newspaper. It is an Arabic newspaper, and it was distributed all over the United States, the Middle East, and Europe. I was very impressed.

The publisher asked me if I would like to represent his newspaper in Arizona, and automatically, I replied yes. They were willing to train me and pay for a course in journalism. I am a person who does not say no to knowledge. I took the course and started writing for the newspaper. I represented it in Arizona, and I did a great job.

Al Wasat Al Arabi went out of business. I began writing for *Anba Al Arab* in Arabic. I had interviews with very famous poets and men of literature from the Arab world.

Later I began to write in it in English in compliance with the many requests I received. I started covering stories of charity work and all of the activities of St. Jude Hospital, delivering to the people acts of love and compassion. In my writing, I directed the attention of the readers to the significant meaning of love and compassion. I wanted the reader to know that love still exists in this world and that people still help one another. I said to myself, *How can I spread the word of God and make people get along using the power within?*

XIII

I started writing about meditation and positive visualization, and it worked perfectly. People were very happy with what they were reading because I made an overture to the Arabic culture through the positive visualization: a new way to approach God and how to be able to forgive and to forget. Still, it was not enough for me. Even with all of these things that I learned, I needed to get more education, more knowledge, and more insight and, most importantly, to be closer to God.

One day, I was reading the *New Age* magazine. Turning it's pages, I noticed an advertisement by the University of Metaphysics. It offered home study, from a bachelor degree to a doctorate degree, and I said to myself, *Oh, that is what I am looking for.* I copied down the phone number and the address and wrote to them. Within a week, they sent me a packet of information. I opened the package and discovered that this was the link that was missing in my real dreams. This is what I wanted. The God within me directed me in buying this magazine. It was meant for me to see that advertisement.

XIV

In His creativity, God said, "Let there be light." Was God living in darkness before He uttered that phrase? Positively no. He used the light as a symbol of knowledge, of freedom, and of love.

The infusion of man's consciousness of God illumines to man the purpose of his life and the attainment of the truth he seeks. This truth will be his freedom, but when? Only when he realizes the purpose of his life and when his dormant consciousness starts to wake up. It will happen when the cloud of unknowing is blown away by the winds of knowing, making space for the flood of light to invade mind's mansions. This cloud curbs his harmony with his own self, with others, and with the universe. In the absence of harmony, man is detached and separated. He lives in aloofness, and on top of it all, he is fettered. All these shackles deprive his life from love, and with the lack of love, peace is lost. It is this inner light that reveals the Omnipresent to us. Tagore writes in "Sadhana," "When this light is lighted, then in a moment he knows that man's highest revelation is God's own revelation in him." He adds by saying, "And his cry is for this—the manifestation of his soul, which is the manifestation of God in his soul."

Man attains levels of perfection when he realizes that his soul has communed with the infinite. It is the revealing of the infinite through the finite. He can also feel the union of the Supreme Will and Love with his own will and love. Such a state of consciousness would place the aspirant on a new plane of existence, a plane of elation and joy, a new sense of eternal life.

It is in fact the final step that one may attain in existential oneness with the ultimate truth. It is true that the number of aspirants are increasing. All seek to know more and more about yoga, mysticism, meditation, and metaphysics. Such a goal should be pure by itself in order to fulfill the end the aspirant is seeking. When guided by love and will, the individual will be able to free himself from past karma to transcend all barriers.

St. Augustine says in this connection, "My mind with the flash of one hurried glance, attained to the vision that which is . . . but I could not sustain my gaze; my weakness was dashed back, and I was relegated to my ordinary experience, bearing with me only a loving memory, and as it were, the fragrance of those desirable meats on which as yet I was not able to feed."

No one can tell exactly what the aspirant may attain, but one thing is certain: the object of his discovery is one with the object of his quest. The time has come for all schools, universities, and educational institutions to introduce into their curriculum "meditation" as a required discipline, to be practiced by the students before starting their lessons. Meditation is a way of life, self-discipline, control, and concentration. The main thrust of its exercise is to breathe, and through breathing, the meditator acquires the energy he needs. It purifies the lungs, establishes peace and harmony, and helps the mind to be fresh and alert. It keeps the unity between all students strong.

Besides these fruitful yields, we have indicated previously other therapeutic qualities accomplished by healing. Below are some of them:

(a) Strengthens the nervous system.

(b) Stimulates some of the body's organs.

Meditation should be practiced early in the morning and before going to sleep. Certain physiological changes take place in these times in the morning. The body is refreshed by sleep, at night, again the body is relaxed.

The conclusion of all my reading and the spiritual growth that I have attained up to this point in time is the secret door to success in overcoming grief, tragedy, difficulty, loss, low self-esteem, lack of self-control, confidence and self-discipline. All the books of meditation, yoga, and positive visualization helped me. The more knowledge a person has, the more the awareness becomes limitless.

Christopher Hills says in his book, *Success Is A Way Of Life,*

> For the great, failure does not exist. Each failure is just another lesson in a great and mysterious spirit working through evolution. The great evolutionary intelligence itself, which gives us our brains, our genes, our bodies, has turned all its mistakes into successes, all its millions of failed sperms and eggs and seeds into the triumph of the one seed that germinates. Fertilize one egg and it will produce hundreds more that can be destroyed over and over without affecting its power to reproduce itself.

The universe bestows this power on anyone who can lift his mind and consciousness up into the realm of enthusiasm, for this one quality is infectious to others. If even one cell of our body can be saturated with the spirit, it can intoxicate all others around it.

If you find even one cell of your body that can send out the signal of enthusiasm, you can be a success. For success does not depend on money or fame or name, but on your ability to summon up bliss in the midst of pain, to know love in a world seething with hate. Success is joy and laughter and lightness of heart in the midst of heavy burdens. Success is the ability to carry the world's problems on your back and yet feel that "the yoke is easy and the burden is light." All these silent friends helped me. Yes, these are my silent friends who helped me in my solitude and comforted me. In a very gentle and enlightening way, they showered me with information that I was seeking and yearning.

I continued my life's journey through spiritual growth and enlightenment, leaving behind the unconsciousness and limitations of the human condition. Through the teachings of my beloved guru, Paramahansa Yogananda, I was able to discover how to cope with grief and the loss of a loved one and how to deal with life in general. I learned how to concentrate and focus my mind and achieve awareness of divine joy and peace. His teachings guided me into learning to have inner and outer balance and how to banish darkness and ignorance thru proper breathing, exercises, mental calmness, and deep concentration for profound mediation.

These steps made a difference for me:

1. Take time to heal, one day at a time. Healing is growth. It is all right to feel up one day and down the next.

2. It is okay to feel or to be helpless, empty, angry, guilty, lacking motivation, lacking energy, and lacking appetite.

3. All feelings are part of the process of recovery.

4. Remember that there is a purpose for everything that happens in this life.

5. Always remember that you are strong, intelligent, loving, caring, responsible, beautiful, whole, and complete.

6. Tomorrow is a new day, and you are getting stronger and will overcome this loss.

7. Reading is essential for the healing process and to learn how to cope with the loss.

8. Meditate. It is very beneficial to the mind and body. You will get answers.

9. Learn to exercise. One of the greatest exercises is yoga because it is an exercise for the body and the mind.

10. Set goals for yourself. You achieve whatever your dream is.

11. Stay away from addictive substances such as alcohol, drugs, cigarettes, etc.

12. Remember always: the universe loves you, and your powers are within. You are the captain of your ship.

13. Where there is a will, there is a way.

14. Stay away from thinking negatively. Avoid depressive situations.

15. Take long walks. Nature is a natural healer.

16. Wake up early in the morning, receive the new day, and see how the sun smiles at you.

17. Start something creative and easy.

18. Learn how to breathe properly. The breath is the cord that connects the soul to the physical body.

19. Be silent and still. In stillness is where you can find God (love, peace, joy, and harmony).

20. Always remind yourself not to be limited. The entire universe lies within you. You are infinite, just like your Heavenly Father.

21. On a daily basis, remember to thank the Omnipresent for his gifts.

METAPHYSICS

Metaphysics is the branch of philosophy that deals with all questions of matter, mind, and spirit through thought. The Reader's Digest dictionary defines "metaphysics" as "the branch of philosophy that investigates principles of reality transcending those of any particular science, traditionally including cosmology and ontology." The word "meta" originates from Greek, which means "after" or "beside" or "with"; hence "metaphysics" is the science that is beyond "physics." Meditation to metaphysics is like the branch to the tree. Hence, the above prelude was a must. The inquirer may ask what is "thought"? Again, we have to advise the dictionary. Here below are some of the definitions:

1. The act or process of using the mind actively and deliberately

2. Meditation

3. Cogitation

4. Intellectual activity of a specific kind

And what is the "word"? It is a signal, a communication, a message. It is the "thought" and the "logos." "In the beginning was the word and the word was God." We must deduce that in the beginning was the "message," which is God's thought to man. In the beginning was God, which was "life" and "truth." In the beginning was the thought and the inner knowing—the Inner All-Knower.

Down through the ages, man tried to seek his position in the "Universe-God." Since then, he never ceased asking, "Who am I?" Man is but God's image on earth. Man then partakes in the nature of his Creator, yet God is universal and man is an individual. Through this understanding, man is able to live this "energy" and to practice it in his daily life and activities.

Philosophers and thoughtful men such as Bacon, Descartes, and Aristotle believe that the existence of beings apart from the sensible world of matter and change can be demonstrated and that something can be known of their nature—whether they are called immaterial substance, spirits, and intelligence or God and souls. Spinoza holds that "the human mind possesses an adequate and infinite essence of God." He maintained that man's highest good is his "knowledge of the union existing between the mind and the whole of nature."

Hence metaphysics seeks wisdom about ultimate realities. This confirms what Aristotle says: "Metaphysics is the wisdom that deals with the *first* causes and principles of *all things*" (emphasis added). He adds, "Though physics also is a kind of wisdom, but yet, it is not the *first* kind." He also says, "Both physics and metaphysics must be classed as parts of wisdom."

Physics deals only with material things in motion and "the mathematician" investigates abstraction—objects which, except as abstracted, cannot exist apart from matter and motion. He also added, "If there is something which is eternal and immovable and separated from matter, clearly the knowledge of it belongs to a theoretical science, not, however, to physics, nor to mathematics, but to a science prior to both."

But according to Plotinus (AD 205-70), "It is a dialectic and it is the most precious part of philosophy, because it transcends reasoning and argument, and it is through it, a person attains the truth, even without expressing any word." Metaphysics is considered by theologians as a supernatural knowledge, "the divine gift to man of a contemplative wisdom to which his nature cannot attain by its own unaided powers."

Bacon, in *The Advancement of Learning*, makes the following distinction: "We must note that physics regards the things which are wholly immersed in matter and morale, so metaphysics regards what is more abstracted and fixed; while physics supposes only existence, motion, and natural necessity, whilst metaphysics supposes also Mind and ideas . . . As we have divided natural philosophy into the investigation of causes to theory, which we again divide into physical and metaphysical, it is necessary that the real difference of these two be drawn from the nature of the causes they inquire into." In other words, metaphysics means the hidden wisdom, in which a searcher tries to attain to and to realize it perfectly through his nature. At a certain stage, man discovers the spiritual will is above the ethical life and defines his actions accordingly. Such an attainment means that man is conscious, that he is "above mind." Oscar Wilde, in his novel *The Picture of Dorian Gray*, says, "The aim of life is self-development. To realize one's nature perfectly—that is what each of us is here for."

So meditation is one pole of our terrestrial conscious activity, which is "all-creative." It is an experimental exercise that involves man's individual actual attention and *not* belief system or other cognitive process. "Zen is looking at things with the eye of God; that is, becoming the thing's eyes so that it looks at itself with our eyes. But, this is not enough. Impressions must always be accompanied by expressions. Impression without expression is not yet impression. Expression without impression is impossible. But impression and expression are not enough. Expression without reception is meaningless. It is not expression if it is to nobody. This is why all art, all music, all poetry require two persons. Why only two? How can you ask for a word when even two minds with the same thought is almost unheard of?" (Blyth).

The meditator's aim is to attain a psychological state known as "transcendental awareness" defined by the Orientals as *satron*. Holmes says, "God governs not through physical law as a result, but first by Inner Knowing, then the physical follows." Vann says, "The heart of man is hungry for the reality which lies about him and beyond him . . . a hunger not to have reality but to be reality." While Dayson says, "The mind, I believe, exists in some very real sense in the Universe. But is it primary or an accidental consequence of something else? The prevailing view among biologists seems to be that the mind rose accidentally out of molecules of DNA or something similar. I find that very unlikely.

"It seems more reasonable to think that the mind was a primary part of nature from the beginning manifestations of it at the present stage of history. It is not so much that the mind has a life of its own, but that the mind is inherent in the way the Universe is built, and life is nature's way to give the mind opportunities it would not otherwise have."

So the mind is more likely to be primary and life secondary rather than the other way around. In other words, the "mind" has the capability to control and to govern, to a certain extent, the functions of the body. All man's conditions are controlled by the mind—which is the *law*—and they is always an *effect*; and in our lives of conditions, we are the *cause*.

God is the energy giver, and our souls are *vibrant*. We are God's children who crave to merge with their Creator. We vibrate because we have a mind that governs the body's vibrations, which is the thinking process (including the subconscious thinking); and through our consciousness, we come into contact with the universe. Mind and experience, its aspects—the divine inflows into consciousness from the individuation particles of God's universe—these experiences are known as the insight, inspiration, and intuition. Meditation is the window through which we can perceive the spirit in us. But that is still not sufficient, nor even thinking spiritually is sufficient. For to be spiritual, one has to live as a spiritual being as spirit is the energy that one lives by and the body has to express it.

Schwarz says, "Every act of our lives should be an act in which we realize that it is the spirit that moves us in its broadest sense. Whatever levels of growth we have achieved, we must try to act in this way if we are to be spiritual."

Man's aim concentrates on how to enlarge his consciousness and to feel that truth is all-comprehensive, attained through the interpretation of one's being into all objects, and realizing harmony flowing between his spirit of the world, his individuality, and that of the universe.

He will then be able to discover and realize the unity of the world with the conscious soul of man, which unity is contained by the eternal spirit whose power

a. created all things;

b. illumines the mind—our mind—with consciousness and awakens the sense of responsibility; and

c. realizes the wholeness of *his existence*, his relation with all, through his union with God, the Infinite.

Man comes to realize the following:

a. In union, and not in what he possesses, lies his power.

b. He needs to learn how to cultivate his sentiment with life's sympathy by detaching himself from all worldly things.

c. He must free himself from all distractions, shackles, and barriers. Man loses all his originality and other attained qualities when he is deprived of his self-realization. His spirit diminishes; it loses its radiation and loses, in consequence thereof, his *inner knowing*.

For what is self-realization save the permeation of his being and his unity with the all-pervading Spirit—"the breath of his soul." In addition to these losses, he will be bereaved of his harmony with nature. He will be enslaved when he prides himself over others and binds himself to worldly pleasures, centering his aim on material things. In this case, his possessions become his shackles. He becomes limited with them. His comprehension narrows to the borders of these limited possessions, and the distance between him and the Infinite Being becomes infinite.

Yogan-Gaibi says, "Becoming a slave to superficial self, don't think you become a king; be a slave to the King of Love: that's what kinship is."

In the teachings of Buddha, we read, "With everything, whether it is above or below, remote or near, visible or invisible, thou shalt prepare a relation of unlimited love without any animosity or without a desire to kill. To love in such a consciousness, standing or walking, sitting or lying down till you are asleep, is Brahma Vihara, or in other words, is living and moving and having your joy in the spirit of Brahma." The Upanishad explains the spirit as the being whose essence is the light and life of *all*, who is *world-conscious*. To attain world-consciousness is to unite our feeling with the infinite feeling and to be fully conscious of the reality of *all*. A person has to free himself from all worldly bonds and personal desires.

The Upanishad says, "Thou shalt gain by giving away."

Man gains every time he gives away, but he should not give for the only reason that he will be rewarded, but rather, because in giving away, he is fulfilling a human aim. However, Gibran in *The Prophet* says,

> And there are those who give with pain, and that pain is their baptism.

> And there are those who give and know not pain in giving, nor do they seek joy, nor give with mindfulness of virtue;

> They give as in yonder valley the myrtle breaths its fragrance into space.

> Through the hands of such as these God speaks, and from behind their eyes He smiles upon the earth.

We are close to the end of the twentieth century. Man's life is becoming so miserable. Crime is at its highest level. Materialistic values are replacing the real values. Man is living in a horrible chaos, a miserable hell. He lives a blind and artificial life. All his worries, distresses, troubles, pain, and tensions are due to his immersion in a world of materialism. He is enslaving himself and adding more and more shackles and barriers to his soul. He is degrading his human species (one of the 8,400,000 other species) that exist on this earth (the plants, the birds, the beasts, the insects, the fish, the aquatics). How is he delivered from this chaos, from this pit of darkness? What is the way to restore the lost peace to his troubled soul and mind? How does one draw himself back to harmony, the constructive force of the universe? The only solution that might save him and restore his tranquility and peace of mind is through meditation.

The wise Lao Tse used to pray, "God, Lord of the Universe, heap not worldly gifts at the feet of the foolish men. Give me the gift of the untroubled mind."

Where there is God-consciousness, we unite ourselves with God. We feel his presence at a specific location. We read in the Psalms, "Seek peace and pursue it." We also read, "Righteousness and peace have kissed each other."

Kabir, the saint of India, writes,

The mirror is within the heart

Still you cannot see The face of the Lord

His face you will perceive

When your mind is free.

And in John, we read, "Peace I leave with you, my peace I give unto you: not as the world giveth, give I unto you. Let not your heart be troubled, neither let it be afraid."

The peace of mind, the inner peace, is the most precious gift that man is rewarded with, and who else but himself who rewards it to himself. All other gifts are nothing. They are useless. They have no value. Their only value is the imagination that one prizes them. They are good only for their vainglory. It is a fake and artificial glory that taints one's life with its vanity and its artificiality.

Meditation is the bridge of man's salvation. It is man's life elixir. Even when Tagore writes his poems, he meditates. He meditates in his own way. We read in one of his poems,

> I will utter your name, sitting alone among the shadows of my silent thoughts.

> I will utter it without words. I will utter it without purpose.

> For I am a child that calls its mother a hundred times, glad that it can say "Mother."

Even the well-known mathematician and poet Omar Khayyam sought meditation in his own way. He symbolized his poems that were misunderstood by the readers until they had been revealed in the explanations and clarifications made by Walters as he understood them from his teacher Paramahansa Yogananda:

And lately by the Tavern Door agape

Came stealing through the Dusk an Angel Shape

Bearing a Vessel on his Shoulders; and

He bid me taste of it, and 'twas the Grape!

In his explanation to this stanza, Walters says, "Lately after deep meditation, and while still the door of silent intuition stood ajar, there stole through it an angel of God's consciousness bearing with him a vessel of beautiful wisdom. 'Drink,' he requested me, and I did taste. Ah, wonder of wonders! It was the nectar of heavenly bliss."

Kabir glorifies meditation in one of his songs. He says,

Go to heaven—why go back to earth?

In the house of the fearless one,

Where music, unstruck, sounds,

You shall play trumpets.

. . . .

Unfettered meditation brings salvation:

Your heavy load is taken off.

. . . .

Meditation will free you from dependence on others:

. . . .

Your life will blossom:

Deeply drink this meditation.

When man is wakened, he goes on seeking for truth. Out of all the species on earth, only man has the power to understand truth. Truth is mind's liberation; and when one man is freed, he attains the pure joy. His freedom is achieved by

1. losing one's ego;

2. uniting himself with all others;

3. uniting himself with the universe;

4. being in harmony with nature and others; and

5. experiencing the joy of unconditional love.

For in love we are strengthened and are given a hidden power that was unperceivable from before. In this respect, Gibran says,

> Like sheaves of corn he gathers you unto himself.
>
> He threshes you to make you naked.
>
> He sifts you to free you from your husks.
>
> He grinds you to whiteness.
>
> He kneads you until you are pliant;
>
> And then he assigns you to his sacred fire, that you may become sacred bread for God's sacred feast.

Meditation develops in man virtues of tenderness, patience, and humanism. Meditation acts as a dispelling factor to negative emotions, which are real causes to several and different types of illnesses and diseases. Negative emotions act as a hindering element between the body and its commending self. It expands our growth and increases our comprehension and cognition. It expands the realm of our love to universality and through it, we achieve the following:

1. The doors of empathy and true understanding are flung open.

2. Our insight becomes sharper, putting our thoughts to work, hand in hand with our actions, and seeking all the unity in purpose and finding their joy. This has been well explained in the Upanishad: "Only those of tranquil minds and none else can attain abiding joy, by realizing within their souls, the being who manifests one essence in a multiplicity of forms."

3. Love is freedom in action. When a person seeks something transcending itself, it means that he is seeking for his freedom; and when he is freed, he defeats the "ego," the selfishness, and all worldly desires.

4. Love is the highest level of life's perfection.

Attaining this means man's soul has attained the unconditional love whose magnetic force acts in the opposite direction of the negative forces; and through the fire of this love, oneself is totally freed, and in this freedom, it comes to realize its higher self, reflecting thereby its goodness to society's welfare.

The desires of the physical body that is self-centered could be abated by one's consciousness merged in love. They work in combination toward all goodness, enjoying truth, love, and infinite joy and realizing perfection through this harmonious sympathy. For truth is infinite; its opposite is but a shade that is soon effaced.

Man aspires to a vision that links society's harmony with all its surroundings. When this is actually realized, then each member of the concerned society could view things far better than before and will always be thrilled by the results. One of the old wise sayings says, "Our spirit finds its larger self in the whole world, and is filled with an absolute certainty that it is immortal."

And one of the seer poets sang, "From love the world is born, by love is sustained, towards love it moves, and into love it enters." And, "God is love, God is truth, God is infinity; God is the beginning and no end and where you are, God is, so God is everywhere."

Again, the Upanishad teaches us, "Man becomes true if in this life he can apprehend God; if not, it is the greatest calamity for him."

When a person knows that whatever is in the universe is filled by God—God is Love—and whatever one may possess are God's gifts, he realizes the "infinite in the finite."

Rumi, the Iranian mystical poet, says, "Love is the astrolabe of the mysteries of God." When we realize the God-consciousness, we come to realize also that our true image is the image of God.

Bhajan says, "Eyes are the light of the soul, ears are the instrument of the divine, the tongue is the creativity of the creator. This is the trinity which makes the totality of God-consciousness." He added, "Be one with the divine: that is the ultimate Cosmic Energy in which you are to merge." He also added, "You shall have the light within you, light equal to that which you cannot say." By light, it is meant the happiness, the peace, the joy, the freedom from all borders—the inexpressible "in words" of pure and real ecstasy.

Omar Khayyam says, "Both heaven and hell lie within you," and Tolstoy, the Russian writer says, "The kingdom of heaven lies within you." When we seek the goodness, then all that is good is reflected on us, and the contrary is also true.

Baker, in her famous book, *Science and Health*, says, "Beauty as well as its truth is eternal, but the beauty of material things passes away, fading and fleeting as mortal belief. Custom, education and fashion form the standards of mortals. Immediately, exempt from age or decay, the *radiance of soul* has a glory of its own. Immortal men and women are models of spiritual sense, drawn by perfect mind and reflecting those higher occupations of loneliness which transcend all material sense" (italics mine).

She also wrote, "Few deny the hypothesis that intelligence, apart from man and matter, governs the Universe and it is generally admitted that this intelligence is the eternal mind and divine principle, love."

1. It generates energy.

2. It leads to self-determination.

The meditator has to stop his meditation when he feels that he is:

1. tired and/or distracted or nervous,

2. suffering a headache or any bodily illness, and

3. when negative thoughts invade his mind.

Meditation is the healing power to many illnesses and diseases. But this mainly takes place after a period of time.

When a meditator is taken beyond his senses, then beyond his mind, he begins to experience something of this transcendent reality; when this experience grows gradually, it begins to affect his whole attitude toward others and toward the universe itself.

Krishna tells Arjuna in the Gita, "With an atom of myself, I sustain the Universe."

The Islamic Sufis believe too that all the world and the cosmos is wrapped within oneself: "Thinks't you are minor planet!! though the greatest world lies within you."

This is an implication of the fact that the most valuable and most adorable thing in the world, in the cosmos, is man, and only man has the God-powers, being himself the *image* of God.

EPILOGUE

All religions teach and agree that God created us through his breath.

Because of our state of dream-like-reality, we forget our true nature and amuse ourselves with material things.

Our ignorance lead us to believe that our body is sustained by food and water. It is the Breath that sustains the body. We are the "soul."

Confronted and torn by sorrow, sadness and regret, we try to understand what befell us.

It's time to wake up from our nightmare with all the misery it hatches: pain, grief, sorrow, hunger, disease, desire, greed, competition, envy, jealousy, confusion, resentment, expectation, disappoint , restlessness, dispute and war; being all the grass-roots of ego.

When we attune ourselves with our true nature we realize that all creation is governed by the one and only energy; "God's Breath." There is no separation.

We are the eternal soul and not the body,

We are the facets of the diamond and its sparkles,

We are God's breath.

Furthermore we realize that the secret mystery of Life and Death is the absence of death. And that which exists is only Life. And that which perishes is the flesh and the bones.

To the Reader

A heart-filled thanks and appreciation to you, the reader. Words cannot express, how grateful I am that you chose *Unveiling the Mystery of Life and Death*. I hope this book has inspired and enlightened you. It's because of your support that my dream will come true. All proceeds from the sale of this book will go toward building God's Little Children Orphanage.

Love and light,
Dr. Sylvie Daniel Bidot

Donations may be deposited under the bank account of:

GOD'S LITTLE CHILDREN ORPHANAGE
Account# 723105276
CHASE JP MORGAN BANK
Phoenix, Arizona, USA

To contact the author by mail and email:

DR SYLVIE D BIDOT
P.O.BOX 71268
PHOENIX AZ 85050

DRSYLVIEB@AOL.COM

REFERENCES

Bacon, Francis. 1605. *The Advancement of Learning*. (Publisher Unknown).

Bhajan, Yogi. 1977. *The Teaching of Yogi Bhajan*. CA: Arcline Publication.

Bloomfield, Harold, and others. 1975. TM-NY: Dell Publishing Company.

Chitrabhanu, Guruder Shree. 1978. *The Dynamics of Jain Meditation*. NY: Dodd, Mead & Co.

Colgrove, Melba, Harold H. Bloomfield, and Peter McWilliams. 1991. *How to Survive the Loss of a Love*. CA: Prelude Press.

Dass, Nirmal, trans. 1991. *Songs of Kabir*. Albany: State University of New York Press.

Eddy, Mary Baker. 1934. *Science and Health*. Boston: Trustees under the Will of Mary Baker.

Ellfeldt, Louis. 1980. *Dance from Magic to Art*. Iowa: Wm. C. Brown Co., Publishers.

Evans, Wentz W. Y. 1969. *Tibet's Great Yogi Milarepa*. USA: Oxford University Press.

Forem, Jack. 1976. *Transcendental Meditation*. NY: E. P. Dutton & Co. Inc.

Franck, Frederick. 1978. *Zen and Zen Classics: Selections from R. H. Blyth*. USA: Vintage Books.

Gawain, Shakti. 1978. *Creative Visualization*. CA: Whatever Publishing Inc.

Gibran, Kahlil. 1923. *The Prophet*. NY: Alfred A. Knopf Inc.

Goldsmith, Joel S. 1986. *Collected Essays of Joel S. Goldsmith*. CA: DeVorss & Company

Heidegger, Martin. 1961. *An Introduction to Metaphysics*. NY: Doubleday & Co.

Hills, Christopher. 1983. *Success Is a Way of Life*. USA: Microalgae International Sales Corporation.

Hoffman, Enid. 1981. *Huna: A Beginner's Guide*. Pennsylvania: Whiteford Press.

Holmes, Ernest. 1957. *Creative Mind and Success*. NY: Dodd, Mead & Co.

Johnston, William. 1973. *The Cloud of Unknowing*. NY: A Doubleday, Image Books.

Le Shahn, Laurence. 1984. *How to Meditate*. NY: Bantam Books.

Lear, H. L. Sidney. 1918. *Hidden Life of the Soul*. London: Longmans, Green & Co.

McDermott, Robert A. 1970. *Radhakrishnan: Selected Writings on Philosophy, Religion, and Culture*. NY: E. P. Dutton & Co. Inc.

McKean, Richard. 1947. *Introduction to Aristotle*. NY: Modern Library.

Ouspensky, P. D. 1971. *The Fourth Way*. NY: Vintage Books.

Pelletier, Kenneth R. 1977. *Mind as Healer, Mind as Slayer.* NY: Dell Publishing Co. Inc.

Peterson, Severin. 1971. *A Catalog of the Ways People Grow.* NY: Ballantine Books.

Prabhavanda, Swami, and Christopher Isherwood. 1955. *The Song of God Bhagavad Gita.* NY: Mentor Books.

Prabhavanda, Swami, and Fredrich Manchester, trans. 1957. *The Upanishad.* NY: Mentor Books.

Ray, David. 1979. *The Art of Christian Meditation.* NY: Pocket Books.

Rolle, Richard, trans. 1981. *The Fire of Love and the Meaning of Life.* NY: Image Books.

Russell, Bertrand. 1957. *Mysticism and Logic.* USA: Anchor Books Edition.

Shah, Douglas. 1957. *The Meditators.* NJ: Logos International.

Shapiro, Deane H. 1980. *A Scientific Personal Exploration Meditation.* NY: Aldine Publishing Co.

Schwartz, Jack. 1977. *The Path of Action*. NY: E. P. Dutton & Co. Inc.

Sechrist, Else. 1972. *Meditation*. Virginia: ARE Press.

Shunn, Florence Scovel. 1925. *The Game of Life*. CA: DeVorss & Co.

—. 1945. *The Power of the Spoken Word*. CA: DeVorss & Co.

St. Clair, David. 1975. *Instant ESP*. NY: New American Library.

Staudacher, Carol. 1987. *Beyond Grief*. CA: New Harbinger Publications Inc.

Tagore, Rabindranath. 1922. *Sadhana*. NY: McMillan Co.

Tolstoy, Leo. 1961. *The Kingdom of God Is within You*. USA: Noonday Press.

Lao Tse. 1995. *The Book of Meaning and Life*. England: Penguin Books.

Underhill, Evelyn. 1955. *Mysticism*. NY: Noonday Press.

Vail, Elaine. 1982. *A Personal Guide to Living with Loss*. NY: John Wiley & Sons Inc.

Webster's Family Encyclopedia. 1988. NY: Arrow Trading Company Inc.

Walters, Donald J. 1994. *The Rubaiyat*. CA: Crystal Clarity Publishers.

Wood, Ernest. 1994. Concentration: An Approach to Meditation. DL: The Theosophical Publishing House.

Yagan, Murat, and Diane Wilson, trans. 1994. *Gaibi*. Vernon-Kebzeh Publications.

Yogananda, Paramahansa. 1990. *How You Can Talk with God*. CA: Self-Realization Fellowship.

Zachner, R. C., trans. 1992. *Hindu Scriptures*. London: J. M. Dent & Sons Ltd.

Dr. Bidot's mom and dad with Uncle Edward and
Auntie Maria

The mom and Dad of Dr. Sylvie Bidot Mr. Louis
Daniel and Mrs Louigina Daniel

Grandma Luigina Daniel with Richard

Grandpa Louis Daniel with grandson Richard

Grandma Luigina and grandson Richard

Valentina with her Grandpa Louis Daniel

Dr. Sylvie Bidot and her father Louis Daniel

Richard and Valentina, 14 years old and 6 years old

Richard and Valentina

Dr. Sylvie Bidot with Richard and Valentina

Dr. Sylvie and her children Richard and Valentina

Dr. Sylvie Bidot with her son Richard

Dr. Sylvie Bidot with her daughter, Valentina

Richard age 4 ½

Richard age 4

Richard age 5

Richard age 8

Richard, Dr. Bidot's son. 8 years old.

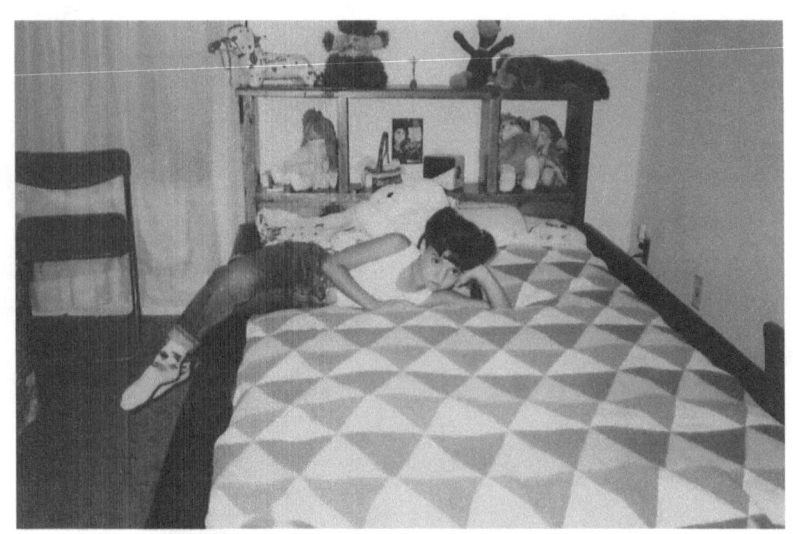

Valentina Bidot 5 years old

Valentina Bidot, 6 ½ years old.

Valentina Bidot, 6 ½ years old.

Valentina, age 6

Valentina Bidot, 6 ½ years old.

Dr Bidot, Robert and Valentina

Dr. Sylvie, Valentina and Robert Bidot

Valentina Bidot 25 years old

Valentina Bidot 25 years old

Valentina Bidot 26 years old

Valentina Bidot age 27 years old

Valentina Bidot age 27 years old

Dr. Bidot and her husband Robert wedding day

Dr. Sylvie Bidot and her husband Mr. Robert Bidot

Dr. Sylvie and her husband Robert.

Dr. Bidot

Dr. Sylvie Bidot with First Lady of Lebanon, Mona Hraoui

Dr Bidot and Tipper Gore, the wife of the former
US Vice-President

Dr. Sylvie Bidot, Vice President, wife Tipper Gore
and the prominent and respected Eddie Basha,
founder of Basha's Food Supermarkets

"Life is a rainbow of experiences. Beneath it lies eternal bliss."

Out of her tragedy, the author shoot up her
thought's sprouts and sprinkled them with
the light emanating from her inner soul,
embracing thereby the peaks of inner self
beauty.

—Najwa Salaam Braks,
a well-known writer,
translator, and poetess

The author succeeded in picking the right key
in unlocking a secret that occupied man since
his existence on earth.

Another caliber of Her success in this book
is the power of transforming one's life in a world
seemed to be endangered by many a faulty
defect in one's society, including the wave of
one's clinging to personal and collective
individuality that breeds competition, hatred,
dispute, violence and war.

—Yousef Abdulahad
(a well-known Arab Writer and an author)